Masterpiece Theatre

Masterpiece Theatre

An Academic Melodrama

SANDRA M. GILBERT
—— *and* ——
SUSAN GUBAR

RUTGERS UNIVERSITY PRESS
New Brunswick, New Jersey

Frontispiece: From "Great Moments in Lit-Crit,"
by the *VLS* Editors, drawn by S. B. Whitehead,
Voice Literary Supplement, October 1988.

Library of Congress Cataloging-in-Publication Data

Gilbert, Sandra M.
Masterpiece theatre : an academic melodrama / Sandra M. Gilbert
and Susan Gubar.
p.   cm.
Includes bibliographical references.
ISBN 0-8135-2182-3 (alk. paper)—ISBN 0-8135-2183-1
(pbk.)
1. Literature—History and criticism—Theory, etc.—Drama.
2. Criticism—United States—History—20th century—Drama.
3. United States—Intellectual life—20th century—Drama.
4. English teachers—United States—Drama. 5. Canon
(Literature)—
Drama. I. Gubar, Susan, 1944–   II. Title.
PS3557.I34227M37   1995
812'.54—dc20   95-5458
CIP

British Cataloging-in-Publication information available

Published by Rutgers University Press, New Brunswick, New Jersey
Manufactured in the United States of America

In Memory of Elliot L. Gilbert
(1930–1991)

Contents

Introduction

The Charges of the Cultural Brigades, the Dilemmas of the Excluded Middle

The Sea of Faith
Was once, too, at the full, and round earth's shore
Lay like the folds of a bright girdle furled;
But now I only hear
Its melancholy, long, withdrawing roar. . . .

And we are here as on a darkling plain
Swept with confused alarms of struggle and flight,
Where ignorant armies clash by night.
    —Matthew Arnold, "Dover Beach"

Two weeks before the 1992 presidential elections, warfare dominated the headlines: the aftermath of the Gulf War, the escala-
tion of the civil war in what was once Yugoslavia, the ongoing
strife in Somalia, the hostilities in the former Soviet Union, the
shadow of conflict in America's inner cities, the three-sided
battle between Bush, Clinton, and Perot (with its persistently
military rhetoric)—and the so-called culture wars. On a day in
early November, we found ourselves at a conference of feminist
critics, all of whom were as obsessed with international, civil,
economic, political, and cultural warfare as we were. Several of
our colleagues, indeed, had just returned from stints on the
hustings, where they were campaigning either for Clinton or
for some of the surprising number of women candidates for the

INTRODUCTION

Senate and the House. But, given our mutual commitment to academia and our professional engagement with the humanities, most of us were especially absorbed in questions about the impact that a change in administration might have on the future of higher education.

If Clinton were elected, whom would he appoint to head the National Endowment for the Humanities and the National Endowment for the Arts, and would his appointments significantly change the atmosphere in which the culture wars had been waged? Perhaps even more crucially, would a Clinton presidency not only revive our failing economy but do so in a way that would be healthy for increasingly imperiled and impoverished university humanities programs around the country? We all knew graduate students who couldn't get jobs, departments that had been reduced or cut, undergraduates who couldn't get into the classes they needed or who were funneled into huge lecture courses, fellowship offerings that had been discontinued, research funds that had been obliterated, publishers whose lists had been drastically pared. At the same time, we suspected that in (or perhaps because of) this atmosphere of gloom, even nihilism, the headline-grabbing "culture wars" had become both more ferocious and more absurd than when the first shots were fired by William Bennett and Allan Bloom in the mid-eighties.

Most recently, the culture wars have been analyzed and editorialized by a range of journalists and scholars, including Gerald Graff (in *Beyond the Culture Wars*, 1992), David Bromwich (in *Politics by Other Means: Higher Education and Group Thinking*, 1992), Robert Hughes (in *Culture of Complaint: The Fraying of America*, 1993), and Harold Bloom (in *The Western Canon: The Books and School of the Ages*, 1994). Their predecessors on the intellectual battlefront included Charles J. Sykes (in *Profscam*, 1988), Lynne Cheney (in *Humanities in America*, 1988), Roger Kimball (in *Tenured Radicals*, 1990), and Dinesh D'Souza (in *Illiberal Education*, 1991). But the hoariest warriors on the field were surely Bennett, whose belligerent *To Reclaim a Legacy* appeared

Introduction

in 1984 when he was President Reagan's secretary of education, and Allan Bloom, whose irascible *The Closing of the American Mind* hit the *New York Times* best-seller list in 1987.

Why did the first salvos in this battle of the books ring out when they did? At the time, we barely understood what was going on, but lately the political roots of the culture war have become increasingly clear. As Robert Hughes points out, in the early seventies Nixon's then-speechwriter Pat Buchanan sent his president a telling "memo on the uses of divide-and-conquer politics: 'If we tear the country in half, we can pick up the bigger half' " (Hughes, p. 45). But by the time Bennett and Bloom loaded their canons for action, such politics had become diversionary as well as divisive. Whether consciously or not, these intellectual captains of conservatism understood that it was in the interest of a Reaganite government to divert attention from the ills of society, while dividing and conquering a confused public by scapegoating a small group of academics for problems over which that group had little or no control.

Are Mom and Dad worried that Johnny and Janie can't read? Blame the literacy problem on a few deconstructionists at Ivy League universities, thereby deflecting attention from reductions in funding for K–12 education. Do Henry and Henrietta Heartland find themselves nervous and anxious on the streets of cities increasingly filled with ethnically diverse populations? Single out academic proponents of multiculturalism for attack, thus distracting the Heartlands from the real implications of social change. Have the Heartlands become unnerved by homelessness, illegitimacy, crack babies? Blame "liberationist" ideologies for problems that would otherwise be clearly associated with poverty, and in particular with a widening gulf between the haves and have-nots. Does Dad find himself vexed that Mom has to work so the Heartlands can make ends meet? Explain that the culprit in this situation is a cadre of radical feminists operating out of the Ivory Tower rather than an economy whose imperatives encourage the formation of two-income families. Are the Heartlands irritated by the conspicuous consumption they envy in upper-middle-class yuppies, by the narcissistic wonderland of arbitrage and junk bonds, by the me-first credos of therapy groups and exercise salons? Tell them that such selfishness stems from the "identity politics" promulgated on campuses all over the country before they can notice that me-first is actually the national policy propounded by the Reagan administration itself. Have the baby boomers—and particularly the sixties New Left—evolved into a significant voting bloc? Contain and control their political potential by castigating a few Marxist and/or feminist professors.

Like many intellectuals, we barely understood the dynamics of this situation when it began to develop in the mid-eighties. In fact, we initially responded to Bennett's and Bloom's battle cries with a mixture of contempt (What could a reactionary Republican like Bennett possibly know about the kind of work we and our colleagues really did?) and indifference (Why should, or would, any sophisticated humanist attend to the curmudgeonly rantings of an eccentric philosopher?). But, again like many intellectuals, we eventually found that these war whoops were impinging on our lives as writers, readers, and teachers, no matter how we tried to ignore them. From *Newsweek* and *Time* to *The New Criterion* and *The American Scholar,* low-, middle-, and highbrow magazines featured articles caricaturing or lambasting an academy that we hardly recognized from our own experience. And, as if internalizing such misrepresentations, many departments we inhabited, visited, or evaluated began to split along lines determined by such largely fictive critiques.

The closing of the American mind? The opening of the American mind? What was the (*was* there a) truth of the matter—and could it, *how* could it, be told? In the late eighties, an engaged and engaging group of concerned administrators, whom we encountered at a Washington, D.C., conference of state humanities commissions sponsored by the NEH, implored us to challenge the neoconservatism advocated in *The Closing of the American Mind* by defending the egalitarian projects of women's studies, black studies, and other interdisciplinary endeavors in a piece that should, they proposed, be called "The Opening of the American Mind." Others, too, as we traveled around the country in what we now consider our salad-bar days on the lecture circuit, consistently (and often plaintively) wondered whether we, or anyone, might be willing to leap to the defense of new humanistic methods and projects whose practitioners seemed oddly disinclined to explain themselves to the general public. Until the early nineties, after all, much commentary on the culture wars was provided by hostile journalists whose "research" had been mostly funded by highly partisan right-wing organizations.

But despite the intensity with which colleagues around the country sought to enlist spokespeople in the culture wars, we began by finding ourselves surprisingly alienated from the rhetoric of both sides in these contemporary debates, this even though we knew that we were deeply committed to intellectual innovation, to feminist and African-American studies, to new methodologies and egalitarian pedagogies.

Such alienation, in fact, appeared particularly odd in view of our realization that the neoconservatives actually thought we (and our friends) were the villains! Yet despite our growing awareness that attacks on the academy were usually trumped-up efforts to mystify real social problems (problems with solutions far more complex than the simplistic solutions proposed by, say, Bennett or Bloom), we were surprised to find ourselves, at times, strangely sympathetic to parts of the neoconservative arguments and to some of the values on which those arguments were founded.

Why did we feel as we did? How embarrassing! And how could we dramatize our discontent with the terms of the debate and still remain true to our position in the debate itself as well as to our convictions about the joy of reading, the pleasure of writing, the historic centrality of the book, and the future responsibility of educators?

"This is all just like a soap opera," we exclaimed in 1989, laughing at ourselves, each other, and our quandary.

INTRODUCTION

And so we wrote a soap opera, an "academic melodrama" about cultural changes both in and out of academe, about the politics of higher education and the poetics of the literary marketplace. Our twin themes: faced with a world of theoretical and antitheoretical passion, mercantile exploitation, and cynical devaluation, what can a poor text do? Similarly, confronted with the same constellation of material or immaterial conditions, what can a poor assistant professor of English do?

Could she, for example, simply enlist on one or another side in the battle of the books that has now been waged for almost a decade not just in scholarly journals but also in bestsellers, popular magazines, and TV talk shows? Or would she, like us, find herself curiously bemused and bewildered by the very nature of the controversy? Might she agree with past and present NEH heads Bennett and Cheney as well as academic humanists Allan Bloom, E. D. Hirsch, and Helen Vendler that our students lack fundamental knowledge about the touchstones of art and history? Yet wouldn't she also have profited from the attacks on the nature and status of that knowledge mounted by semiotic and reader-response critics (for instance, Robert Scholes, Stanley Fish, and Richard Ohmann), by African-American specialists (for example, Henry Louis Gates, Jr., and Houston Baker, Jr.), and by feminist critics (among them, Lillian Robinson and Jane Tompkins)?

Let's call advocates of the Bennett and Bloom position the "Back to Basics" platoon: this contingent tends to use words like *excellence, universality, transcendence, disinterestedness,* and *greatness* to argue that the writings of Plato and Shakespeare, Milton and Keats embody core "truths" of Western civilization, truths that teachers should transmit as a legacy to students. In the view of these thinkers, the villains who have threatened to splinter and politicize the humanities are obscure specialists or politically correct, left-wing ideologues, all of whom speak to each other in incomprehensible jargon. Therefore, the Back to Basics proponents present themselves as defending a body of knowledge that should constitute a stable curriculum, expressing humanistic wisdom—expressing, indeed, the highest aspirations of the Western tradition—against the onslaughts of the new barbarians.

From the perspective of their antagonists, however, the Back to Basics group would return us to a basically white, middle-class, and masculinist definition of culture. The position of these critics, whose battle cry we might label "Forward into Instability," should not be viewed as monolithic, for, like one of those charmingly varied platoons featured in old World War II movies (the Italian from the Bronx, the WASP from Kansas, the black from Alabama, etc.), *this* group includes feminists, new historicists, and Marxists as well as theorists of gay studies, reader-response critics, and African-American scholars. Disparate though they are, however, the members of the Forward into Instability contingent consistently use such words as *relativism, indeterminacy, multiculturalism, diversity,* and *historical specificity* to argue that new bodies of knowledge should be included in the curriculum and, more specifically, that literary tests written by hitherto marginalized peoples are crucial objects of study, as are the products of popular culture in past and ·present societies. In the view of these thinkers, the villains who threaten to turn the humanities into irrelevant anachronisms are "naive essentialists," "patriarchal old boys," and "ethnocentric elitists," all exploiting the public's distrust of a discourse it does not understand.

We ourselves would expand and supplement such name-calling critiques with a number of observations. To begin with, it strikes us that the Back to Basics group is not only elaborating a not-so-secret political agenda, but is also inappropriately homiletic. Where the originators of the Great Books concept usually wanted students to read, say, Plato so that they could learn to think for themselves, the Back to Basic Training army wants students to read Plato so that Plato can think *for* them. In other words, rather than defining *The Symposium* as a work to be challenged, engaged, or studied for its historical significance, these warriors consider it a sort of sermon in stone, a

INTRODUCTION

monument of unaging intellect to be unquestioningly wor-
shipped as a source of timeless ideas and values.

Despite their ostensible homage to history, therefore, the
proponents of Back to Basics are oddly ahistorical in their insistence on a rigid and naive perpetuation of supposedly transcendent truths as well as in their nostalgic allegiance to a mythical
Golden Age in which, so they imply, there was once a proper
understanding of, and respect for, the relationship between
tradition and the individual talent. Whatever *Was,* evidently,
Was not only Right but Better. Clearly, then, whatever was *not*
but now *is* or is coming into being must be wrong. Thus new
ideas, new books, new reading practices, new intellectual populations—all are disparaged, excluded, or ignored.

Considering that we ourselves have long been committed to
a range of academic innovations, why should we feel any affin-
ity whatsoever with this cadre of regressive and traditionalist
thinkers? What attracts us, at least in part, about the Back to
Basics group is that, despite the arrogance of their attacks on the
new, a notable modesty shapes their attitude toward works of
art, authors, history, and the function of criticism at the present
time. Most humanists, after all, came to work at the university
precisely because they were inspired by a love of art, authors,
history—and most began their scholarly careers with a desire
both to illuminate and preserve the past. To the extent that the
Forward into Instability platoon has jettisoned any concept of
aesthetic greatness, their Back to Basics antagonists provide a
healthy corrective, reminding us that there really is a difference
between explicating Keats's "Ode on a Grecian Urn" and analyz-
ing a telephone directory, just as there is a difference between
teaching Emily Dickinson and teaching Danielle Steel.

In addition, to the extent that the innovative ideas of recent
theorists are all too often couched in trendy and obfuscatory
jargon, the relatively lucid treatises produced by Back to Basics
commentators are refreshingly accessible, reminding us that if
we wish to have any palpable effect on our culture, we in the
academy need to realize what Adrienne Rich has called "the

dream of a common language." Finally, to the extent that—in different ways and with different purposes—members of the Back to Basics camp do define cultural literacy as a political good at least theoretically available to all, our teacherly selves have to sympathize with a project that takes seriously the notion that students from a range of diverse backgrounds will profit from an understanding of the great books that have shaped their own cultural inheritance.

To be sure, the Forward into Instability group would claim that in its own fashion it, too, seeks to recuperate our cultural inheritance. Yet if we align ourselves for a moment with the position taken by Back to Basic proponents, we find a number of flaws in the strategies of some deconstructionist, feminist, African-American, popular culture, and new historicist scholars. Despite their skepticism toward monolithic, fixed interpretations of the cultural past, a notable hubris or chutzpah shapes the Forward into Instability attitude toward works of art, authors, history, and the function of criticism at the present time. Elevating the significance of critics and their interpretations over and against that of authors and literary works, many practitioners within this school privilege theory and metacriticism over serious textual interpretation. Not only do artist and art get lost in the critical shuffle, but critical self-fetishization is often cast in an uncommonly jargon-ridden, even incomprehensible, idiom.

Equally troublesome, though the metacritical idiom of the Forward into Instability party is often sprinkled with terms of a lexicon drawn from an ostensibly interdisciplinary range of humanistic approaches—derived, for example, from philosophy, psychology, or linguistics—much of the scholarly and pedagogic work produced in such supposedly multidepartmental studies features only the veneer of an interdisciplinary methodology. (Political scientists frequently don't recognize the Marx of Marxist criticism; psychologists scoff at the Freud constructed by psychoanalytic criticism; philosophers often scorn the Wittgenstein, the Heidegger, and the Nietzsche

INTRODUCTION

valorized by deconstructionists; historians sometimes chuckle at the history produced by literary "new historicists.") Often, too, the theoretical vocabulary of one prominent (usually French but sometimes German and more recently Russian or Polish) thinker reappears over and over again in a host of different books, articles, and reviews, but the fashionable "discourse," together with the hypotheses on which it is based, quickly devolves into a dreary argot that threatens to take on the status of revealed truth. With so much attention focused on *au courant* contemporary theorists, therefore, it is hardly surprising that some of the teaching and scholarship produced by this congregation of academics has been marred by a parochial ahistoricism: teachers schooled in recent theory display arrogance and ignorance about even those aspects of the aesthetic past that have shaped their own ideas while focusing, almost to the exclusion of most other subjects, on increasingly rarefied "postmodern" phenomena.

Why, then, do we tend as a rule to identify more closely with the Forward into Instability platoon than with the Back to Basic battalion? Obviously, of course, the work we ourselves do, like the work done by our antitraditional cohorts, is based on a consciousness of the *politics* of reading, writing, and canon revision. Just as obviously, the democratization of the curriculum to which our colleagues are committed is founded on an awareness that hidden assumptions about race, class, and gender have skewed, indeed deformed, the cultural "legacy" to which such thinkers as Bennett and Bloom would like us to pledge allegiance. In addition, however, we cannot help being engaged and excited by the innovative energies the Forward into Instability group brings to humanistic studies, by the imperative to read both traditional and nontraditional texts in interesting ways, and by a renewed attention to aesthetic theory that refuses to take anything for granted, even (or perhaps especially) Plato's or Aristotle's monumental sermons in stone.

Do we represent a kind of intellectual "excluded middle,"

an academic silent majority that seeks to find a way out of the darkling plain on which the culture war's impassioned armies clash by night and day? A mathematician friend recently reminded us that Gödel's theorem proposes that the excluded middle may be exactly the right place to be, since certain propositions can be neither true *nor* false—and maybe culture warriors can therefore be both right *and* wrong. Curiously enough, indeed, a number of paradoxes and blindspots link the Back to Basics camp with the Forward into Instability proponents, deconstructing what are usually perceived as inexorably opposed binaries.

Paradoxes:

- The so-called elitist right actually uses a "common language," but the so-called revolutionaries deploy an elitist jargon.
- The so-called advocates of cultural literacy as a political good don't believe, as do those who scoff at "cultural literacy," in the democratization of the curriculum and of academic institutions in general.
- Although the Back to Basics battalion claims to honor the achievements of great artists and although the Forward into Instability company expresses admiration for the (postmodern) pleasures of the text, both groups are strikingly alienated from the real practices and producers of the arts—poets, painters, playwrights, composers, novelists, sculptors, filmmakers: for the traditionalists, alas, it appears that the only good artist is a dead artist, while for the radicals the only real artist is the critic-theorist.

Blindspots:

- Both sides in the culture war remain, for the most part, blind to the real needs and problems of real students, that is, to the crisis in literacy that means the very processes of reading and writing are probably more important at this point than the culture war's questions about what is to be read and what is to be written.

- Both groups appear largely ignorant of the major new ways in which scientific knowledge—the knowledge that is for the most part acquired and promulgated in the university but outside the humanities—might impinge upon the knowledge(s) that are the staple of the humanities: C. P. Snow's old problem of the "two cultures" not only lives but prospers in this atmosphere of in-fighting and alienation. (As a corollary of this, in fact, both groups are equally indifferent to the existence of other nonhumanistic areas in the university—communications, media studies, journalism, business, marketing—all of which are not only competing with them for shrinking resources but also dislodging traditional departments from centrality.)

- Both groups, too, seem largely unaware of the absurdity their skirmishes take on in a larger culture dominated not by deconstructionists or traditionalists but by Madonna, Michael Jackson, Michael Jordan, McDonalds, and Mitsubishi.

- Finally, and perhaps worst of all, both groups act as if the economics of education were irrelevant to the humanistic enterprises they advocate. For what does it mean, really, to treat these issues as if they were not inexorably affected and inflected by the faltering job market for undergraduates and graduate students alike, the shrinking budgets of universities everywhere, and the general financial climate of a country sunk in the doldrums of unemployment, homelessness, rising health care costs, and a corroding industrial infrastructure?

We earlier mentioned the "silent majority"—a rather opprobrious phrase from what Robert Lowell once called the "tranquillized *Fifties*"—but we would like here to redefine this term so that it represents academia's silenced and excluded middle, the group to which we believe we ourselves really belong. Logically, as members of an excluded middle, we seek to find a *middle ground* or *common sense* that could unite the best of what both sides proclaim in the culture wars. Practically— that is, pedagogically—as members of this excluded middle we consider (as many of our colleagues also surely do) that our own deepest allegiance, and our profession's, should be to students and their needs, needs neither for indoctrination in Plato nor for indoctrination in Derrida, but rather for an appreciation of the ways in which the dynamics of the past shape the innovations of the future.

Personally, however, our own insight into the paradoxes and blindspots we've outlined here led to a bemusement and amusement, a horrified hilarity, that triggered the composition of our farcical *Masterpiece Theatre: An Academic Melodrama.* And given the history we've been discussing, we set our comedy of academic manners in the late eighties, when the culture wars had begun to escalate alarmingly and, as it was soon to appear (in the light of a flagging economy), absurdly.

Act I of *Masterpiece Theatre,* "The Perils of the Text," focuses on the battle between Back to Basics and Forward into Instability educators, factoring in media portrayals of the stars of academe. Significantly, as we try to show, what accompanied the late eighties hype about inflated claims from both sides of the battle of the books, lending it an eerie (if not sinister) resonance, was the decrease in funding of humanities research initiated by the Reagan administration, a product of more general Reaganite cutbacks in the moneys allocated to education. And in Act II, "Foreign Intrigues," we trace a similar situation in England: a schism between conservative preservers of humanistic knowledge (Alistair Cooke, George Steiner) and Marxist, poststructuralist theorists (Terry Eagleton, Toril Moi), a breach that widened even as government support of higher education in England was being eroded during the Thatcher years.

Two other theoretical positions in the Forward into Insta-

INTRODUCTION

bility group, both highly influential in contemporary English departments, also concern us in "Foreign Intrigues," namely the impact of so-called postcolonial criticism and of deconstructive theory, and once again, we seek to explore odd juxtapositions in the evolution of these intellectual movements. Curiously, the opening of the canon to postcolonial literature and criticism (represented here through the projects of Edward Said and Gayatri Spivak) occurred at a time when fundamentalist strains of thought surfaced both in the States and in the Middle East, posing a direct threat to free expression (as in the Salman Rushdie case). Strangely, too, deconstruction (fathered by Jacques Derrida in France and Paul de Man in America) seemed to liberate the text or even history itself from any single, authoritative meaning, or so its emphasis on indeterminacy implied. But the revelation of De Man's pro-Nazi writings during the early forties posed a crucial question: was the notion of indeterminacy itself merely a mask to hide the problems of the past? If so, what intellectual contradictions does this imply for French feminist re-inventors of deconstruction (Hélène Cixous, say, or Luce Irigaray or Julia Kristeva)?

Just as important, what influences do the ideas of Marxist, postcolonialist, Derridean, and feminist theorists exert on American undergraduate education? What is their attitude toward the nature of the literary text? toward the existence of real authors? In Act III, "The Final Deletion," we consider the situation of artists in the literary marketplace today. From Marshall McLuhan to Alvin Kernan, social observers have suggested that what was once a powerful culture of print seems to be disintegrating as one-time readers—including most of our students (and even many of our colleagues)—increasingly put aside their books and turn on their TVs, VCRs, CDs, and PCs. Examining, on the one hand, the commodification of the work of art by writers, agents, publishers, and publicists and, on the other hand, the forces of censorship generated by the political right and left, we explore the transformations of literacy and cultural literacy in a society that markets, packages, and recycles products of the imagination and their producers with as much hype and sleaze as it sells all other consumer goods.

Thus, though we begin in the heart of the heart of the country with "Campus Capers," we travel in *Masterpiece Theatre* on "The Eurocentric Express" to the continent of fashionable intellectual theory and then return to the New York literary scene of "Bookworms in the Big Apple," where we confront stars of the written word (Norman Mailer, Stephen King, Kathy Acker), stars of the lecture stage (Robert Bly, Camille Paglia, Allen Ginsberg), and stars of the big and little screen (Madonna, Shirley Maclaine, Michael Jackson). Throughout our journey, we encounter figures in the political arena (Nancy Reagan, George Bush, Jesse Helms), all of whom illuminate the social contexts that necessarily exert powerful pressures on professors and their students, writers and their readers.

The fate of the text and of aspiring teachers of English hangs in the balance. Will the text, as we have known it, survive campus feuds, theoretical debates, political attacks, economic exploitation, and media manipulation? Will the humanities, and in particular the profession of English, endure as a recognizable discipline, transform itself, or slide toward extinction in the future world of letters? Will the future even include a world of letters?

Meditating on change, its problems and its possibilities, at that preelection conference in November of 1992, we realized that everything we write here is provisional, hypothetical. The Clinton administration struggles to support the economy, to energize the citizenry, to implement a health care plan, and to solve problems of funding for higher education while coping with Republican backlash at the polls and in Congress, and the parameters of the problems we confront may well expand or contract. As this book goes to press, for example, we have witnessed the astonishing spectacle of two former NEH directors (William Bennett and Lynne Cheney) testifying against the agency they themselves administered. Clearly, the social, intellectual, and even technological issues implicit in the culture

INTRODUCTION

wars will be with us for some time to come, no matter who or what slouches toward the White House to be born(e). For amid the charges and counter-charges of the culture wars, the words of the immortal (albeit dead white male) Tennyson, in his classic (if retrograde) "Charge of the Light Brigade," remain pertinent: "Someone ha[s] blundered!"

As we brooded on such blunders, our plots were aided and abetted by a range of individuals and institutions. To take institutions first, we are grateful to the Modern Language Association, to *Critical Inquiry,* to the University of Chicago, the University of Wyoming, New York University, and Eastern Washington State University for providing us with arenas of performance and publication. In addition, as always we are indebted to the support provided by our home institutions, the University of California, Davis, and Indiana University. We also wish to express our gratitude to Leslie Mitchner for her editorial enthusiasm and inventiveness, and to our agent, Ellen Levine, for her warm support. Among individuals, we wish to thank John Beckman, Jonathan Culler, Shehira Doss Davezac, Alice Falk, Stanley Fish, David Gale, Henry Louis Gates, Jr., Susanna Gilbert, Donald Gray, Robert Griffin, Edward Gubar, Marah and Simone Gubar, Lisa Harper, Katharine Ings, Barbara A. Johnson, Elizabeth Oster, Kate Remen, Chris Sindt, and Jeanette Treiber for various forms of encouragement, assistance, or advice.

But our dedication reveals our greatest debt—to the late Elliot L. Gilbert—whose generosity and wit helped set this project going. He might have thought that the finished version is as serious as, in parts of ourselves, we mean it to be. But we hope, too, that he would have laughed at the jokes.

Masterpiece Theatre

*P*rologue

INTERIOR . An E-"LECTURE" "ROOM" AT LUNAR II, A VIR-
TUAL BRANCH CAMPUS OF THE INTERPLANETARY STATE
OMNIVERSITY (IPSO)

*The year is 2088 MUD (Multi User Dimension). The CURATOR OF
PRINT CULTURE (PC), a PROFESSOR OF PAST MODERN STUD-
IES (PMS), and a SPECIALIST IN ARCHAIC SIGNIFICATION
STUDIES (ASS) are conducting an electronic panel "discussion" as
part of a systemwide "colloquium" at IPSO.*

CURATOR OF PC
What we're about to screen right now may be incomprehensible to some of you out there—but it's an excellent
example of the kinds of issues that concerned intellectuals back at the turn of the so-called modernist, even
*post*modernist century.

PROFESSOR OF PMS
Beginning students in this field should note the characteristic *fin-de-mod-siècle* naivetivity with which questions that were soon to become notably irrelevant were
debated and discussed.
                    (*smiles sardonically*)

PROLOGUE

SPECIALIST IN ASS
(*bridling*)
I tend to disagree with my learned colleague. The semiotics of signification, even (or perhaps especially) in the archaic modes and media we are about to confront, *must* continue to concern us, even in our postprint culture, so that we can reclaim the legacy of the past.

CURATOR OF PC
Obviously I agree. And I would remind our students out there that no matter what planet you're floating on, the *inscriptions* and *imbrications* of print (as they were once so quaintly called) continue to have key significations for all of us, if only because our *zeitgeist*, as it were, has been so powerfully shaped in reaction against them. The motto of our great university may be *Ipso Facto* but that curious artifact the book is nevertheless still a crucial component—a key microminichip, you might say—in our macrocultural system.

PROFESSOR OF PMS
To be sure, to be sure. I do of course take your point, especially because the action in the narraspeculation we're about to view—three episodes of what used to be called a docudrama—take place (though of course no one then knew it) just before the Clinton (r)e.volution supplanted the ancient and unwieldy so-called culture of print with the vast network of electronic highways, byways, and flyways that makes everything in today's world possible, from *ipso* to *facto*.

SPECIALIST IN ASS
Nostalgia buffs will instantly recognize that our presentation is drawn from that popular old teleseries "Masterpiece Theatre," which was one of the first, albeit crude, efforts to translate print into more intelligible imagery.

Prologue

PROFESSOR OF PMS

Primitive indeed, but remember that at the time this series was (ahem) *filmed,* the simplest technologies of hypertext and virtual reality were as yet unavailable to ordinary transmitters and transmittees. Nor of course had Gutenbei conceived the electronic implants that allow us, today, to inscan what were once defined as texts.

CURATOR OF PC

For some of us, as you know, the old textologies continue to have considerable charm. Letters on a page! Book jackets! Bindings! They're a different and fun way to enter the virtual reality of the past.

PROFESSOR OF PMS

Oh absolutely, if that sort of thing lights you up. And I'll bet some of these episodes of "Masterpiece Theatre" have already hit the fanscreens out there.

SPECIALIST IN ASS
(*eagerly*)

Pretty soon somebody may even remaster these episodes of "Masterpiece Theatre" for electronic inscanning!

PROFESSOR OF PMS

Unlikely, I imagine—but hey, we can never know what new technologies are waiting in the wings, *can* we?

All three chuckle as the Curator of PC flicks a switch and the old theme of Masterpiece Theatre *rises in the E-lecture studio.*

ACT I

The Perils of the Text; or, Campus Capers

LONG SHOT OF A BOOK-LINED WALL

VOICE-OVER

We'd like to do a little hypnosis on you today. Imagine that you're ensconced in your own family room, your study, or your queen-sized bed. Settling back, you pick up the remote, flick on the TV, and naturally you turn to PBS. This is what you see.

<u>INT</u>. ALISTAIR COOKE'S LIVING ROOM SET

Hosts are seated in front of a roaring fire.

HOST 1

Good evening. Welcome to *Masterpiece Theatre*. Because Alistair Cooke is away on assignment in Alaska, we've agreed to host the show tonight, and that's both a pleasure and a privilege because our program this evening marks the beginning of a fascinating new series, a first on television: *Masterpiece Theatre* will present you with a docudrama entitled "Masterpiece Theatre."

HOST 2

Like "The First Churchills," this show analyzes the situation of real-life people—tonight, most of them in the academy. Names have not been changed to protect either the innocent or the guilty, but all the situations are fictive and at times words have been put into the mouths of people who did not speak them. Other lines, however, are direct quotes from various written sources, although none of the characters, as we depict them, should be confused with any "actual" persons, whether or not these persons would ascribe to the idea of their own reality. Like "Upstairs, Downstairs," this program will introduce you to a spectrum of characters from many walks of life. What's different about tonight's episode, though, is that all these characters have passionate opinions about the show itself. Why, the very idea of *Masterpiece Theatre* drives some of them to guerilla theatre, others to theatre of the absurd. Yes, you've always already guessed it: we focus tonight on "The Perils of the Text," a drama involving what we used to call humanists—now for some a dirty word—and most of our characters are in deep trouble.

HOST 1

You'll laugh with them, you'll cry with them, you won't believe some of the things they say. But their perplexities, arcane though they may sometimes seem, are relevant to all of us. Though they use peculiar words or phrases—canon, speciesism, phallologocentrism, deconstruction, Syntopicon, transcendental signifier, the political-literary complex—their struggles may (or may not) affect the lives of our children and our children's children. For the thrilling episodes you're going to see tonight and in the weeks to come may (or may not) bear directly on the future of education and the education of the future. So sit back, relax, and enjoy.

ACT I

<u>EXTERIOR</u> . A DARK AND STORMY NIGHT IN 1989

The film opens with a TEXT—hunched and limping—staggering down an empty road in Boondock, Indiana. The only light is the faint gleam of golden arches in the distance, down near the railroad tracks, and, a little nearer, the pale blue glow of TV screens at two houses set back from the road. Behind the Text lurches a shadowy and indeterminate figure of malevolent mien. Inchoate cries and whispers proceed from the unseen lips of the Text as its assailant forces it down a steep embankment toward a railroad crossing at the heart of the heart of the country.

Wielding a knife as keen as logic, the MURDEROUS VILLAIN urges the whimpering Text on, on.

TEXT
AHHH! OHHH!! OY!!!

MURDEROUS VILLAIN
(chuckling to him/herself and pushing the Text)
Get along there, move on down. Ha, ha, now, no one will save the text!

The dialectical pair—master and slave—have reached the fast track at the bottom of the hill.

MURDEROUS VILLAIN
(thuggish, as he or maybe she whips out a great chain of being, or perhaps a chain of signifiers signifying being)
Kneel and pray, pray for your life! Your bondage is my discipline.

As the Murderous Villain knots the Text firmly to the railroad track, we see the trapped Text—almost in the halo of the golden arches— gazing up at the stars. What are the morphemes it is muttering? As the assailant stalks off toward Boondock State University, the cam-

6

era ZOOMS IN *for a close-up, but we can barely hear the sound of a pathetic murmur.*

TEXT
(in bondage)
AHHH! OHHH!! OY!!! Who am I? What do I mean?

INT. WASHINGTON, D.C., AN HOUR LATER

Most of the great capital slumbers peacefully beneath a misty March sky, but a late light burns in one federal building, where a single public official stares intently at a computer screen. Devoted as always to the public good, Drug Czar WILLIAM BENNETT is working late. The camera ZOOMS IN on his desk and scans an urgent memo from one of the NEH's operatives: Rumor has it that a text—title unknown—has been singled out for assassination or deconstruction. Recommend that you take special measures to safeguard all touchstones, masterpieces, and monuments of unaging intellect.

Frowning wearily, his sleeves rolled up, Bennett is compiling a list of texts to be protected by the Secret Service. His orders will go out at the crack of dawn. Names of authors whose works might be likely targets of attack by crazed radicals flash on the monitor. Bennett's muscles tense as his fingers hover over the keyboard. Every few seconds he takes a furtive puff of a cigarette, then flicks its ash into the top drawer of his desk. From a list prepared by one of his most trusted associates, he will delete the names of writers whose texts can be considered dispensable in the long fight ahead. It is a pity that some must go so that others can be preserved, but a commitment to excellence demands tough choices. As the camera moves in, our television screen becomes his computer screen.

    AESCHYLUS. *Expendable. Bennett presses the delete key and the name disappears.*
    ARISTOTLE. *Preservation essential. He presses save and the cursor moves down.*

ACT I

> JANE AUSTEN· *Again he saves.*
> CHARLOTTE BRONTE· *She disappears.*
> EMILY DICKINSON· *Expendable. Erased.*
> FREDERICK DOUGLASS· *Gone.*
> T·S·ELIOT· *Protection required. Saved.*
> RALPH WALDO EMERSON· *Eradicated.*
> SIGMUND FREUD· *Deleted.*

As the camera draws back, we hear the drug czar murmuring under his breath, as if it were a kind of mantra, "Just say no, just say no, if you want to reclaim a legacy, just say no."

INT. THE SAME NIGHT, A QUIET OFFICE IN THE DEPART-MENT OF SEMIOTICS AT BROWN UNIVERSITY

A stately bearded man, also working late, is also seated at a computer. Professor ROBERT SCHOLES is preparing a reading list for his graduate seminar on "Signification and Its Dis-Contents," a course in which he and his students will investigate threats that they fear the federal government itself may soon pose to all texts everywhere. On his desk, too, lies an urgent memo, this one from a double agent at the NEH: Most texts suspected of subversion of American Way of Life! Mass execution expected soon.

Names flash on his monitor, too, and again our TV screen becomes his computer screen. Naturally, however, Scholes never hits the delete button. Instead, his list grows longer and longer. To the names of works by such authors as T. S. Eliot and Ralph Waldo Emerson, Scholes adds a host of titles by other writers, including Umberto Eco, Ursula Le Guin, Michel Foucault, Louis L'Amour, Danielle Steel, Alfred Hitchcock, Alex Haley, E. D. Hirsch—and William Bennett.

Yet still he is not satisfied. As the camera pulls back, he, too, is scowling. Then suddenly his fingers clatter at the keyboard and, as if through an act of Providence, three new titles appear:

8

" ROSES ARE RED."
" KILROY WAS HERE."
" I ♥ NEW YORK."

In case his students should think these texts are not worth saving, he asterisks them and types in an explanatory footnote:
" THE MEANEST GRAFFITO, IF FULLY UNDERSTOOD IN ITS CONTEXT, CAN BE A TREASURE OF HUMAN EXPRESSIVENESS."

EXT. SIX O'CLOCK THE NEXT MORNING, A FAST TRACK AT THE HEART OF THE HEART OF THE COUNTRY
The Text lies bound and writhing in its chains. The assailant has disappeared but two joggers wearing Boondock State sweatshirts, Reeboks, and headbands are taking a morning run on a narrow path beside the track. They are talking animatedly to each other as they run.

JENNIFER
So I go, like, *no,* no way can I do that, and he's, like, you'll fail if you don't, and I'm, *no way,* and he's, okay, you'll fail—

SCOTT
No way, bogus!

The Text gathers it strength and screams. The joggers look startled.

SCOTT
What's that weird noise?

JENNIFER
Gross. Like, there's something on the fast track.

TEXT
(*sobbing quietly*)
Save me, save me, I'm a text, please save me.

9

ACT I

> **JENNIFER**
>
> Awesome.

> **SCOTT**
>
> But what's a text?

> **JENNIFER**
>
> Not sure. Something to do with lit. crit., I think—but how should *I* know? I'm a business major.

> **SCOTT**
>
> Well, it beats me. *I'm* in communications.

The Text strains against the chain of being and utters an inscrutable morpheme.

> **JENNIFER**
>
> Don't touch it. It could be some kind of UFO or alien. It doesn't speak our language. Let the campus police handle it.

INT. AN HOUR LATER, THE MAIN OFFICE OF THE ENGLISH DEPARTMENT AT BOONDOCK STATE

The office is empty except for one Ms. JANE MARPLE, a very junior assistant professor who is frantically Xeroxing handouts for her nine o'clock class. The administrative assistant's phone jangles, and Jane picks it up. Cut to split screen, Jane at one end of the line and OFFICER FRIENDLY of the campus police at the other.

> **OFFICER FRIENDLY**
>
> Gotta coupla students here reporting something tied to the fast track at the railroad crossing near the by-pass. They say *it* says it's a text. What's that? They say maybe somebody in your department would know.

The Perils of the Text

JANE

What do you mean? *What* text? Is there an author there? Are there critics or readers on the scene?

OFFICER FRIENDLY

I dunno, lady. It just says it's a text, and the kids are scared of it.

JANE

Well, what's its genre? What's its period?

OFFICER FRIENDLY

Whaddaya talkin' about?

JANE

I mean, is it a poem, a play, a novel—maybe a graffito? Classical? Romantic? Contemporary? And what's its language? Its style?

OFFICER FRIENDLY

Hey, look lady, I still don't know what you're talkin' about, and I can't be bothered with this business at the moment. We're up to our ears in sexual harrassment cases down here. We don't have time for some weirdo callin' itself a funny name.

JANE
(*thinking*)

My God, the Amtrak trains don't run anymore but a freight train could come through any time!

OFFICER FRIENDLY

That's your problem now. This thing seems to be in your department.

ACT I

<u>INT</u>. FIVE HOURS LATER, THE SAME OFFICE

The secretaries are on their lunch break and Jane is again alone and again on the phone. This time a split screen shows Jane at one end of the line and PHYLLIS FRANKLIN, the executive director of the MLA, at the other. Jane is practically weeping, while Ms. Franklin is leaning forward, looking perplexed and concerned.

JANE

No one here will help, believe me. Either they think I'm crazy or they're on sabbatical or they're at conferences or they're too busy at their word processors to listen. And after all I'm the most junior person in the department! The chairman says I'm exaggerating and he's been teaching for thirty years. He says every text he can think of is safe and sound in the Norton anthologies.

FRANKLIN

Are you a theorist? Do you think you can deconstruct or historicize this text on your own?

JANE

I'm not sure. I've taken a few theory courses but I don't know whether I can handle this situation on my own. The poor text! It was in a state of crisis. It seemed to have amnesia—not to know where it came from or what it was or whether it had ever been in a classroom, an anthology, or one of the mass media!

FRANKLIN
(*gravely*)
This is bad. This may call for a task force or a commission, perhaps even a conference.

JANE

e to lose. That text is stuck! A train

FRANKLIN

some concern to our membership.
rstand that it would take me months
ission or pull a conference together.

JANE
(*brooding*)

e. I'll fax a memo to all the impor-
n think of. I'll even send one to the
all to come to Boondock State right
save the text!

FRANKLIN
(*cautiously*)

. I wish you luck. Maybe we can get
MLA out of it.

.C., AN HOUR LATER

*czar, and LYNNE CHENEY, his successor
from an official White House luncheon.
sions and are studying a fax just handed to
gent.*

BENNETT

"an unclaimed legacy," one of the
an achievement."

CHENEY

My God, it might contain "truths that, transcending
accidents of class, race, and gender, speak to us all."

13

BENNETT

It might ask some of "the perennial questions of human life." It might have been written by one of "the great souls."

CHENEY

It might be by Milton or Shakespeare. It might speak "to the deepest concerns we all have as human beings."

BENNETT
(*pausing and scowling more deeply*)
Then again, it might be just a "handmaiden of ideology." It's well known that "*The Color Purple* is taught in more English courses today than all of Shakespeare's plays combined." But no, no.
(*snaps his fingers decisively*)
We can't risk leaving it there. I suspect I know who's done this.

CHENEY

I bet we both know. The left-wing ideologues, the theorists—they're to blame.

BENNETT

And "the narrow research specialists." And a "loss of nerve and faith . . . during the late 1960s and early 1970s."

CHENEY

"Truth and beauty and excellence are regarded as irrelevant." Have you got a printout of your list of the endangered texts that we've decided to protect?

BENNETT

I've got the list, you've got the funds, let's get an air force jet and take off right away!

INT. DOWNTOWN PROVIDENCE

Professor Robert Scholes and a group of graduate students are seated at a table in McDonald's, with a good view of both Ronald McDonald and the golden arches. Scholes alternately nibbles at a McBLT, lectures, and leafs through his mail as the students take notes.

SCHOLES

To wrap up. The point I was trying to make last week is a general one. "I see the myth of decline as a standard element in conservative ideology, just as the myth of progress is fundamental to liberal ideology." But let's turn now to a more specific topic, the reason why we're here today.

(He hands around napkins.)

The semiotics of fast food is a new and interesting field. Hardly anyone has touched it yet. But you might look at a recent, groundbreaking dissertation: "Ideological Productions in the Food Service Industry." This guy is smart, this guy examines "the juxtapositions, dissociations, emptyings, and condensations of sign relations within the restaurant text." You have to look at the lighting, the windows, the landscaping, the menus, and so forth. For example:

(He leans back and sips a Coke.)

What do those golden arches mean to *you?*

STUDENT 1

St. Louis? What are those arches downtown? Could we be dealing with an allusion? Urbanization on the Mississippi? A Twain reference?

STUDENT 2

Come in under those arches, Huck honey?

ACT I

STUDENT 3

No, no, more political than that. Think of the *gold* in those arches. Clearly a representation of the ideals embodied in late bourgeois monopoly capitalism!

STUDENT 4

I don't know. I think there's something deeper going on here. Gates of heaven? A theological subtext?

As the students begin to argue among themselves, Scholes peruses his mail. Suddenly, he stiffens.

SCHOLES

My God. It's happened. I knew it was coming!

STUDENT 4

What's wrong, Bob?

SCHOLES

A fax from Boondock State. There's a text in trouble, and I bet I know who's responsible.

All the students express dismay and concern.

SCHOLES

It's Bennett, it's Washington, it's the worst kind of conservative censorship. He thinks he's going to save Western culture by gagging critics and trashing texts—except of course for the ones he's chosen "upon political grounds."

STUDENT 2

Jesus. And *he* says he wants "to reclaim a legacy"!

SCHOLES

"The leader who will reclaim a legacy is a potent image, ranging . . . from *The Once and Future King* . . . to Adolf Hitler reviving the spirit of a fallen people by finding suitable scapegoats upon whom to blame their fall." And that text in Boondock is a scapegoat as surely as I'm a semiotician!

(*He rises and tosses the remains of his McBLT into the nearest garbage can.*)

You guys finish up here by yourselves. I've got to go home and pack my *Textual Power*.

EXT. THE POSH POOLSIDE TERRACE OF A HEALTH SPA IN ARIZONA

NANCY REAGAN, IMELDA MARCOS, ELIZABETH TAYLOR, and MICHAEL JACKSON are conversing animatedly while uniformed pedicurists labor over their toenails. In the background, a platoon of ghostwriters are hunched at laptop computers.

NANCY

I agree with you, Imelda. People just don't understand. You need at least two hundred pairs just for official occasions.

TAYLOR

Diamonds are a girl's best friend. Diamonds and Emeralds. Diamonds and Rubies. Diamonds and Sapphires. Diamonds and Raindrops. Diamonds and Rainbows—

NANCY
(*ignoring her*)
Did you ever notice what clunkers that Maggie Thatcher wears! She looks as if she has hooves.

ACT I

GHOSTWRITER 1, a Frank Sinatra look-alike, approaches Nancy Reagan deferentially.

GHOSTWRITER 1
Mrs. Reagan, I just got a strange piece of e-mail from Lynne Cheney's so-called hairdresser, you know, the gumshoe who checks out NEH grant writers to make sure they're not gay or feminist weirdos. . . . There seems to be a mysterious text tied to a railroad track somewhere in the middle west.

NANCY
So? Why bother me about it? Can't you see that Imelda and I are having an important private conversation?
(sighs)
Well, as long as you're up, hand me that mirror over there. I can't move with these cotton swabs between my toes.

GHOSTWRITER 1
(handing her the mirror)
Well, but Madam, what if that text is—

NANCY
(interrupting as she peers into the mirror with a look of pleasure)
Still the fairest of them all.

GHOSTWRITER 1
What if it's that unauthorized biography we've been so worried about—*I'll Have It My Way: The Steamy, Seamy Life of Nancy Reagan?*

IMELDA
(reassuringly)
Don't worry. All publicity is good publicity.

NANCY
(*nervously ignoring her*)
Oh God. What if it's another damned book by one of my rotten kids? Or one of Ronnie's lousy whelps?

JACKSON
(*leaning back in his chair with a beatific smile, clutching his crotch, and singing out*)
"I want to love you, pretty young thing. I want to love you, P.Y.T."

TAYLOR
Not a bad idea, Michael darling. Maybe you should call up that nice Lisa Marie Presley and ask her out.

IMELDA
Let them read *People* magazine! Let them read the *Enquirer*.
(*shouts over to her Ghostwriter*)
Cervantes! Don't forget to add something about how I love it when the people read about me.

NANCY
(*under her breath*)
What a fool!
(*aloud to Imelda*)
Imelda, dear, the less they read the better. I made Ronnie try his best: we cut back on student loans and minority scholarships; we lowered the budget for education; we made ketchup a vegetable for school lunches.
(*to Ghostwriter*)
Maybe you'd better search and destroy that text, Milton.

GHOSTWRITER 1
Don't worry. I'll take care of those Strangers in the Night. I'll give them One for My Baby and One More for the Road.

ACT I

NANCY

And another thing. You might want to put in a line or two in my book about how stupid Barbara Bush really is with all that bleeding heart nonsense about literacy.

IMELDA

And her shoes, my dear.

NANCY

Yes, every pair of them looks as though it came from Florsheim's.
(*impatiently to pedicurist*)
Will you ever be finished, Sappho? I have to wake Ronnie up. It's almost time for his afternoon tapioca. And his afternoon after-tapioca nap.

INT. A TELEVISION STUDIO IN CHICAGO

ALLAN BLOOM, acclaimed author of The Closing of the American Mind, *and Dr. RUTH WESTHEIMER, popular sexologist, are guests on a local talk show. The camera is focused on Dr. Ruth, as she finishes explaining why multiple orgasms aren't always necessary for female pleasure, when Bloom leans forward, pounds on the arm of his chair, and interrupts angrily.*

BLOOM
(*snarling*)
Plato. *The Symposium.*

Dr. Ruth looks bewildered.

BLOOM

He didn't think multiple orgasms were necessary either. And he knew whereof he spoke.

DR. RUTH

(*kindly*)

My dear, you seem troubled. What's the problem?

BLOOM

Don't you know that "Rousseau, the founder of the most potent of reductionist teachings about eros, said that *The Symposium* is always the book of lovers. Are we lovers anymore? This is my way of putting the educational question of our times."

DR. RUTH

I see. I had heard your book was about education, but I discover we are not so far apart. I hear you saying that we are both concerned with what you call eros and what I call sex.

BLOOM

(*gloomily*)

The sexual revolution and feminism. Both annihilating eros, although in different ways. And annihilating eros is annihilating Plato and Socrates—in short, the humanities.

DR. RUTH

(*shocked*)

Oh, my poor dear. What are you saying?

BLOOM

I'm saying that "for the great majority [of students], sexual intercourse [is] a normal part of their lives prior to college, and there [is] no fear of social stigma or even much parental opposition." Why, these students "are used to coed dormitories."

ACT I

DR. RUTH
(*skeptically*)
I see. Although in *my* practice—

BLOOM
No, obviously you don't see. Think of feminism. "Central to the feminist project is the suppression of modesty." But that's not all of it. Think of the effects of rock 'n' roll on our young people.
(*turning purple*)
Think of "a pubescent child whose body throbs with orgasmic rhythms; whose feelings are made articulate in hymns to the joys of onanism or the killing of parents; whose ambition is to win fame and wealth in imitating the drag-queen who makes the music." Think of "a non-stop, commercially prepackaged masturbational fantasy."

DR. RUTH
Yes? Yes? You are thinking of that? You are hung up on that?

BLOOM
Nonsense. I'm thinking about the decline and fall of the humanities; I'm thinking about "how higher education has failed democracy and impoverished the souls of today's students." And "the only serious solution is the one that is almost universally rejected: the good old Great Books approach."

DR. RUTH
Yet you just said that "the educational question of our times" is "are we lovers anymore?" You seem to think there is a connection between sex and the humanities.

BLOOM

Eros, eros, not sex.

(*He waves a fax at her.*)

And I'm neither neurotic nor psychotic. I have the evidence right here. The great American public doesn't know it yet but I'm going to reveal something terrible right here on channel seven. There's a text in big trouble down in Boondock, Indiana. And I have my suspicions—

(*darkly*)

in fact, I have my conviction. A bunch of rock 'n' roll–crazed undergraduates from one of those coed dorms have tied Plato's *Symposium* to the fast track! I understand, too, that there's a McDonald's down the road where lots of teenagers hang out. Have I said enough? As soon as this show is over I'm packing my Syntopicon and going straight to Boondock. And I hope I'll be greeted at the airport with the publicity this major crisis in our culture deserves!

EXT. A SAILBOAT OFF THE COAST OF ORANGE COUNTY, CALIFORNIA

Professors J. HILLIS MILLER, of U.C. Irvine, and HAROLD BLOOM, visiting from Yale, are lounging in the sun. Miller is reading a faxed memo and Bloom, chomping on a cigar, is reciting Paradise Lost *from memory.*

MILLER

(*musing*)

Is it worth a cross-country trip? The vexed text—the text, as it were, "sous rature"—might not even be theoretical.

A great wave sloshes over the side, from the wake of a speedboat, and Bloom looks queasy while Miller grabs the line for the mainsail and continues speaking.

You might say we're living in the "wake of literary theory." And, as Paul used to put it, "the resistance to theory is in fact a resistance to reading."

BLOOM
Not just that, my dear. The text in Boondock has to be strong; the text has to fight for its own life. It may be threatened by precursors or it may have been assaulted by a stronger, later text. You know how those texts are: at best, there's always a "battle between strong equals, father and son as mighty opposites, Laius and Oedipus at the crossroads."

He resumes his recitation of Paradise Lost, *muttering* "Him the Almighty hurled headlong" *as Miller brings the boat about.*

MILLER
We may or may not agree on that point, but in any case the text in Boondock has no doubt been "arbitrarily chosen" and in order to proceed with our theory of reading we can arbitrarily choose other texts to replace that one. We aren't, after all, contemplating the disappearance of God. That's happened already, as has been admirably proved. Although there are some publicity-seekers who talk as though that's what we're up against.

He stuffs the fax into a picnic basket.

BLOOM
(*throwing his cigar over the side*)
You don't need to tell *me* about that, Hillis. You know you're in the presence of a strong precursor whose name has been practically stolen at the very crossroads of the humanities and the Western canon.
(*He laughs bitterly.*)

Why, when people talk about Bloom nowadays, which Bloom do you think they mean?

MILLER
To go or not to go! A good example of metaphysical undecidability. Harold, the answer just has to be indeterminate!

<u>INT</u>. THE SEEDY INNER-OFFICE OF AN OBSCURE NEW OR-LEANS PLASTIC SURGEON

Would-be governor and presidential hopeful DAVID DUKE—in hospital garb and attended by three sycophantic brown-shirted skinheads—is choosing a set of new features from slides the doctor is projecting on a small screen.

SKINHEAD 1
I say we should lynch it. Niggers never die. You said so yourself in that music tape, *Niggers Never Die.* They have to be lynched. It's probably *The Autobiography of Malcolm X.*

DUKE
Hold your horses, Heinrich. It might be *African Atto,* the street-fighting manual for urban blacks that I wrote under the pseudonym Mohammed X in order to collect the names of vicious black militants.

PLASTIC SURGEON
(interrupting as a nose flashes on the screen)
Now I can guarantee you, Dave, that this one is pure Anglo Saxon. Not a trace of the Semitic about it.

DUKE
(fretfully)
Too long, too Yid. Still not Robert Redford enough.

SKINHEAD 2

Let's not lynch it, my leader. Let's gas it. It's obviously the Talmud and, as you have pointed out, Jews "deserve to go into the ashbin of history."

DUKE
(absently stroking his small mustache, as he studies the noses that continue to appear on the doctor's screen)
Dammit. If it's the Talmud, it has to go. Every right thinking, red-blooded American knows that the Talmud is a dirty book "full of things like sex with boys and girls."

PLASTIC SURGEON
(pointing to a turned-up nose)
Now this model is great with blond hair.

DUKE
Are you kidding? That's a nigger's nose. That's not the kind of manly, Aryan feature that belongs on the face of the future leader of the NAAWP—the National Association for the Advancement of White People. That nose looks like it comes from race mixing, which, as we all know, leads to bad teeth, overbite, and damage to "vital organs."

SKINHEAD 3
But what if it's *Finders Keepers,* your advice book teaching women how to please men in bed? I've given every one of my girlfriends a copy of that book and—

SKINHEAD 1
Shut up, Adolf. It's by some kike nigger or some nigger-loving kike.

DUKE

Heinrich is right. Here's our chance to defend our Dixie heritage against crime in the streets, affirmative action, and welfare illegitimacy. You boys better get going, you've got some crosses to burn tonight in Boondock.

(*He points to a straight pale nose flashing on the screen.*)

Whaddaya think, doc? That's the one for me. I'll shave the mustache, bleach my hair, and go national.

He begins to sing cheerfully "I'm Dreaming of a White Christmas."

INT. A PRIVATE ROOM UPSTAIRS IN THE HARVARD FA-CULTY CLUB

Professor WALTER JACKSON BATE, of Harvard University, and Professor HELEN VENDLER, also of Harvard, are entertaining Professor MORTIMER ADLER of the University of North Carolina, over a luncheon of boiled cod followed by Indian pudding. All three look grim.

BATE

As I have pointed out repeatedly, even the MLA has been taken over by these fringe groups.

(*He broods and scowls.*)

Lesbian Chicanas! I imagine a lesbian Chicana separatist may be responsible for this vile deed.

VENDLER

Or, anyway, one of those feminist literary critics; they're "frequently naive" and "vulgar." Indeed, "the vulgarity of some of the recent literary criticism by feminists seems to me a new ingredient in critical writing." Why the text in question may be authored not only by Milton or Keats or Stevens but by the creator of that renowned character Sporus!

BATE
(*nodding sagely*)
Yes, Helen, I too worry about Pope's "Epistle to Arbuthnot," yet there's no saving it. The humanities are in "their worst state of crisis since the modern university was formed a century ago, in the 1880s." No one believes in greatness.
(*He munches his fish mournfully.*)
"That's gone."

ADLER
Gone? Greatness will never be gone! The Great Books must and shall endure! Remember Scott Buchanan's five criteria. What he said in 1937 still holds. The Great Book is "read by the greatest number of persons," "has the greatest number of alternative . . . interpretations," "raises the persistent unanswerable questions," "must be a work of fine art," and "must be a masterpiece of the liberal arts." My *Paideia Proposal* has surely kept these texts alive and will continue to do so. To be sure,
(*He picks disconsolately at his cod.*)
it *is* true that that "doctrinal" elitist Allan Bloom seems to have made off with my Syntopicon.

VENDLER
Neither your nor Bloom's Syntopicon can keep those texts alive when they are being bombarded by the "deplorable" and "repellant" puns, the "punishing" and "slapdash" "amateurishness" of the "garbled literary history" produced by certain feminists I might name.

BATE

(*concerned, to Adler*)

Please, help yourself to some Indian pudding. We might as well eat, drink, and be merry, since the world as we used to know it is coming to an end. Although—although,

(*He brightens as he digs into Indian pudding.*)

that fax *was* sent by a woman, a *junior* woman at a place I've never heard of, some Boondock State University. How do we know who *she* is? Why, she might be one of those lesbian Chicana radicals. That text she's worried about might be some piece of feminist trash. In which case—

VENDLER

(*beckoning the waiter for a glass of water*)

Yes, yes. It might even be one of "Sharon Olds' typically pornographic poem[s]" and that junior woman might be one of those "research assistants" so "amply thanked" by the likes of Gilbert and Gubar in prefaces and acknowledgments. I'm proud to say that *I* never thank *my* graduate students.

She dreamily mixes the cod on her plate into her Indian pudding.

ADLER

(*excitedly*)

It's not likely to be a Great Book, then. After all, "in the Western tradition until the nineteenth century, there simply were no great books written by women, blacks, or non-Europeans." Out of the one hundred and four Great Books from 800 B.C. to A.D. 1900 that I have identified, only two were written by women, none by blacks. Between 1900 and the present, *none* were produced by women or blacks.

ACT I

(*He begins intoning the names of authors on his list.*)
Apollonius of Perga, Tacitus, Nicomachus of Gerasa—
all the works of these sages are protected by my *Paidea
Proposal,* and not just for the elite that Bloom cares
about. American students from all walks of life will
read them from kindergarten on!

He leans back, sighing with relief, as do Bate and Vendler.

BATE
That Jane Marple would never worry about one of
those texts. She's probably a lesbian feminist Chicana
herself.

VENDLER
Those junior faculty types self-destruct eventually. As
I've explained in print, "the most cheering thing, finally, about all political movements is their unsuppres-
sible tendency to splinter." All we have to do is wait
and sustain ourselves.

BATE
(*sighing with relief*)
I think we can dismiss this fax as inconsequential!

EXT. LATE AFTERNOON, THE NARROW PATH BY THE FAST
TRACK IN BOONDOCK

*Jane Marple is sitting cross-legged, knitting a multiply significant all-
purpose garment and interrogating the Text.*

JANE
Knit two, purl two, slip one. I've sent for some famous
people who should be able to help us. I've even put in
a call to the campus health center. They have counsel-

ors there who might make you feel better. But in the meantime, try to remember. Even though it's hard. How do your signifiers feel? Do they mean anything to you? Are they playful? Are they multiply referential? Self-reflexive?

TEXT
(*groaning*)
Traces, just traces. Glyphs. Little black and white marks. Help me.

JANE
Signifying nothing? What about a historical circumstance? Isn't there a circumstance inscribed in you somewhere? Or a gender related to your genre?

TEXT
(*haltingly*)
A material condition. I think I might remember one. Maybe it was en-gendered, maybe it was part of a genre hierarchy. But it's hazy.

JANE
Try to remember. Try to re-member. How about an author? A transcendental signifier? A scene of composition?

TEXT
An author. An author-ity. There *was* one once. But maybe it died. Or maybe it had intentions and I didn't live up to them.
(*turning and tossing in agony*)
I was disseminated, I floated free, I had no subject, I lost my stable center, maybe that's why I've been punished, tied up on this margin!

ACT I

JANE

Well, you've certainly been put in question. But can you still thematize? Close your eyes and try!

TEXT

Thematize! I think I used to have readers who said I did. Some were responsive, some were resisting. I think there was once a scene of instruction in a classroom. Somebody accused me of *just* thematizing and somebody else told me to undo myself. But then there was somebody else who insisted that I had to be strong and fight for my life against other texts. They all kept examining my tropes.

JANE

Were they critics? Did they tell you what to do?

TEXT

Yes, wait a minute! Some of them said I should be asking perennial questions about the human condition.
(*sobs*)
But I don't know whether I did! And besides, there were others who said they'd like me just as much if I were only a mean graffito. And still others wanted me to bear the marks of race, class, and gender. Some of them wanted me to be written in blood or milk. Some of them wanted me to be transcendent, like a great soul, and tell eternal truths. It was all so confusing.

JANE
(*sympathetically*)

I understand how you feel. I used to feel that way myself sometimes, in graduate school. In fact, I sometimes feel that way *now* when I read all the abstract, high-minded debates about the canon and the curriculum and theory. After having taught a real Introduction to Literature class, I wonder who—

(*Looking startled, she stops knitting.*)

Oh my God. What have I done? Why, what if all those humanists I sent for—

TEXT
(*pulsing fretfully*)

Humanist? What's a humanist?

JANE

That's a hard question to answer. But never mind that right now.

(*thinking aloud to herself*)

How ironic! This is just the sort of thing Aunt Jane used to talk about. What Propp would call one of the "helper figures" might be the villain. After all, Aunt Jane always said that you could plumb the depths of iniquity in an ordinary English village—and maybe an English department is just like an English village!

EXT. DURHAM, NORTH CAROLINA, EARLY EVENING

A poolside cocktail party is in progress at the luxurious home of FRANK LENTRICCHIA, a Marxist English professor at Duke University. He and some of his colleagues—among them, STANLEY FISH, FREDRIC JAMESON, EVE KOSOFSKY SEDGWICK, BARBARA HERRNSTEIN SMITH, and JANE TOMPKINS—are gathered to honor Professor HENRY LOUIS GATES, JR. In one corner, a bartender dispenses champagne, cocktails, Chardonnay, and various designer waters. White-coated waiters circulate unobtrusively among the guests, bearing trays laden with pâté de foie gras, caviar, crudités, and oysters Rockefeller.

LENTRICCHIA

Social change. It might be a working-class third-generation immigrant text, speaking out, like me, for social change.

(*He gulps an oyster.*)

Some regressive reactionary essentialist humanist probably tied it up in knots. I'd like to punch that guy out.

FISH

Cool it, Frank. Your comment assumes that each of us now faces the individual choice both of evaluating and responding to this situation; whereas in fact we have all long since been fashioned in our attitudes, and even the possibilities of perception, by the interpretive community into which we have been initiated by processes that left us no choice whatsoever. Therefore we shall certainly do what we will now do, but not in any way that would suggest that we are in fact doing it. Although I might add that I personally won't be surprised by *any* sin—if I may use so theological a term.

LENTRICCHIA

Hey, I know what we're lookin' at. We're lookin' at a crime that is a function of an economic infrastructure screened by an elitist essentialist ideology and controlled by conservative patriarchs like Bennett, Bloom, Bate, you know the type.

(*He broods a moment.*)

And who knows who else they've coopted! Some of these people who call themselves "feminists"—hey, they're essentialists too! They wouldn't know a material condition if it hit them over the head in a dark alley.

(*He clenches his fists.*)

SEDGWICK
(*handing him a strong drink*)
You're on the wrong track, Frank. "Male homosexual panic." That's what leads to the bondage and discipline of the text. In other words, homophobia. The text down in Boondock was probably produced by a gay man, and you know how nervous that would make a hegemonic heterosexual. We're up against the kind of gay-bashing that *really* makes the wheels of the patriarchy go round!

PAN TO *bar, where Gates stands talking in an undertone to the bartender.*

GATES
(*wryly*)
Hey, brother, how come the only black folks in here besides me are you and the waiters?

JAMESON
(*coming over to order a drink*)
Another champagne, please.
(*He turns to Gates.*)
What do you think about this business, Skip?
(*He doesn't wait for an answer.*)
In my opinion, this text is a crucial but subversive embodiment of the political unconscious, and the crime is a sign of the political consciousness that dominates Washington right now.

GATES
More specifically, it's "the black work of art." They're trying to shut it up because it's *signifying* in every sense of the word, it's bilingual, it's speaking the master's tongue with a difference. But it's been bound and

gagged out there, no doubt in the name of the Great Books of Western Civilization.

JAMESON

I couldn't agree more. Although the text in question could be *any* dissident work that doesn't lend itself to idealization by the bourgeoisie. In fact, "American Marxists have clearly recognized that the production and consumption of pleasing, exciting and 'beautiful' stories and images has a specific and very effective role in promoting acquiescence to, and even identification with, the relations of domination and subordination peculiar to the late capitalist social order."

(He finishes his champagne and sets the Baccarat goblet down on the bar.)

If rescued, this text might actually break the fascination of students with the supposedly ideologically neutral Good, True, and Beautiful!

HERRNSTEIN SMITH

(coming up to the bar)

Professor Lentricchia would like another Chivas on the rocks, please.

(She turns soothingly to Jameson and Gates.)

But after all, value is always contingent. Your values are contingent too. "Literary value," as I've said in print, "is radically relative and therefore 'constantly variable.' " And "being not a conviction but a conceptualization, relativism in this sense is not a proselytizing position." Besides, if I may quote myself, " 'the subject'—that is, *any* subject, and there are clearly *many* subjects, and they clearly cannot be considered identical except by being question-beggingly posited as so in some essential, underlying way—has a *particular,* that is, individuated though not in all respects unique, identity/economy/perspective in relation to which the present state of affairs is undesirable or not and, accordingly, also in relation to which she 'makes her choice' that it be otherwise or that it remain the same."

JAMESON
Whodunit, then?

GATES
And what's that text?

TOMPKINS
(*suddenly appearing at his elbow*)
I know what it is. It's a work from popular culture that has been deliberately decanonized because *They* say it lacks "stylistic intricacy, psychological subtlety, epistemological complexity."
(*She begins to weep sentimentally.*)
The brutes! It's probably *Uncle Tom's Cabin.*

LENTRICCHIA
(*impatiently, coming to bar with Fish*)
Where's my drink, Barbara?

FISH
(*turning to Tompkins*)
Have you packed yet, Jane? All set for the airport? All ready for Boondock State?

LENTRICCHIA
Hard to believe, but that's the place to be right now. Where it's at. We *can* break the dominance of the hegemonic scripts that late bourgeois monopoly capitalism has foisted on all those poor wretches down there in the heart of the heart of the country! If anyone can, *we* can. Remember, "we're hot now and everyone knows

ACT I

that. . . . I don't think any other English department in the country can boast of the lineup of home-run hitters we've got here."

FISH

Yeah. "It's analogous to what's happening in the NBA." Guys move around. Finally they get together on an all-star team. Go, team, go!

EXT. A SNOWY ROAD IN UPSTATE NEW YORK

Professor JONATHAN CULLER of Cornell University, battling an early spring blizzard, is frantically driving to the Syracuse airport. As he guides the car over sheets of ice, he dictates to his secretary at the Cornell Society of the Humanities.

CULLER

Take a memo for MLA headquarters. Because "literature [is] a particularly revealing framing of language," we would always want to save this text if it was a "literary" one. But in any case, "if there is a unity to literary studies in this new dispensation it comes not from the canon of plays, poems, and novels but from an attention to mechanisms of signification which can be studied in a wide range of texts and text-like situations." So no matter whether this is a text or a text-like situation, I think it has something to do with signification, and I'm on my way to the hinterlands to make a report to Phyllis Franklin.

EXT. DEEPENING DARKNESS ON THE NARROW PATH BY THE FAST TRACK

Jane is desperately filing at the chain of being (or signification) with an old saw, while the Text, which has lapsed into unconsciousness, thrashes violently against its fetters.

38

TEXT

"I would rather be a cyborg than a goddess"! I would rather be a rhizome with "multiple entryways"! A "*map and not a tracing*"! I don't want to stand by my man and make cookies! I believe in family values! Take away that Coke can!

JANE
(*gasping, to herself*)
O my God, it's having a nightmare.
(*to the Text*)
Wake up, please wake up. Try to be calm. They might be here any minute. If we could only get away to my classroom. Maybe we could meet the counselor from the Health Center there. And some of my students might help us.

TEXT
(*confused*)
I was dreaming. What a strange dream! What is a cyborg? What is a rhizome? Why cookies?

JANE
(*wonderingly*)
I can't imagine. It's as though you've been in some other world. But I want to find out what you mean in this one.

TEXT
(*hopefully*)
Do you mean I have a meaning for you?

JANE
You little fool! I want to save you!

ACT I

(*lovingly*)
And *I* want to save *you!*

INT. A TINY, TWELVE-SEATER COMMUTER PLANE EN ROUTE FROM ST. LOUIS TO BOONDOCK

Forward, in two uncomfortable seats, Professor SANDRA M. GIL-BERT, of the University of California, Davis, and Professor SUSAN GUBAR, of Indiana University, are drinking Diet Cokes. At the rear, Professor E. D. HIRSCH, of the University of Virginia, is chatting with a MEMBER OF THE BOONDOCK HIGH BASKETBALL TEAM who is returning from a college recruitment visit with Bobby Knight at Indiana University.

SG1
I knew we should come. That was *my* idea.

SG2
I thought it was *mine!*

SG1
Don't you remember what I said on the phone the other night?

SG2
I thought *I* said that!

SG1
It might be a blank page on which the "pen [as] penis" has inscribed itself. Worth saving, no? If only for historical purposes.

SG2
Rewriting Bloom again?

SG1

Which Bloom?

SG2

Can you tell the difference? And in any case, what if it's a female-authored text? It might have been stolen from the *Norton Anthology of Literature by Women!*

SG1

Don't be naive. We can't say we think there's a female author. We'll look like fools.

> (*She rattles ice in Diet Coke ferociously and opens a package of honey-roasted peanuts.*)

Do you want *Them* to call us essentialists?

SG2

What's the difference? Otherwise they'll say we're destroying two thousand years of Western Culture! And please stop eating my peanuts!

PAN TO *the rear of the plane, where Hirsch and the basketball player bob amicably together, as the aircraft hits spots of turbulence. They too are drinking Diet Cokes and munching peanuts.*

HIRSCH

Cultural literacy. You'll need that to get ahead in the world. For example, think of a landmark text like *Romeo and Juliet.* Don't be afraid of going to IU. It's "acceptable to take one's entire knowledge of *Romeo and Juliet* from *Cliff Notes.*"

BASKETBALL PLAYER

Romeo and Juliet? One of those foreign movies?

HIRSCH

"*Romeo and Juliet:* A TRAGEDY by William SHAKE-SPEARE about two 'STAR-CROSSED LOVERS' whose

41

ACT I

passionate love for each other ends in death because of the senseless feud between their families. The line 'ROMEO, ROMEO! WHEREFORE ART THOU ROMEO?' is well known."

(*He chomps a peanut.*)

BASKETBALL PLAYER
(*looking stunned*)
Jeez, Coach Knight said we'd have to know things like that!

PAN TO *the front of the plane, where Gilbert and Gubar are looking uneasy as the aircraft descends through high clouds to the small Boondock airport.*

SG1
Who is this Jane Marple, and what does she want?

SG2
Cui bono?

SG1
No, no, she's part of a long female tradition. Her geneal-ogy certifies her. Why, she's probably thinking back through her literary and literal mothers, as Virginia Woolf might say. An act of affiliation, I mean.

SG2
Between Bennett and Bloom on the one hand, and those theorists on the other hand, it's a wonder she's not a madwoman. Maybe she *is* a madwoman?

CUT TO *the rear of the plane, where Hirsch is still talking to the basketball player as the aircraft lands.*

The Perils of the Text

HIRSCH

Just remember: "To be culturally literate, one does not need to know any specific literary texts."

The plane comes to a bumpy halt on the runway at Boondock.

EXT. THE PATH BY THE FAST TRACK

The path is now completely shrouded in darkness except for the small circles of light cast by two flashlights, one held by Jane, the other by a bearded FREUD LOOK-ALIKE.

JANE
(to Text)

This is Dr. Sigmund from the Health Center. We're hoping he can help you find the Real You.
(in an undertone to Sigmund)
I'm afraid this text is in very bad shape. It's started having nightmares and hallucinations.

DR. SIGMUND
(gravely)

Maybe we're looking at a case of texteria—or do I mean testeria?
(turns to Text)
Do you feel comfortable about talking to me?

TEXT
(ignoring him)

I saw cyborgs, I saw rhizomes, I saw pubic hairs on Coke cans, I saw someone who didn't want to bake cookies, I saw someone who kept shouting about family values.

ACT I

DR. SIGMUND

I hear you saying you saw cyborgs, you saw rhizomes, you saw pubic hairs on Coke cans, you saw someone who didn't want to bake cookies, you saw someone who kept shouting about family values.

TEXT
(eagerly)

That's right. And it was a nightmare about Judy, too. Judy, Judy, Judy.

JANE

Who was this Judy?

TEXT

Judy knew the "discursive limits of 'sex.'" She said, "the conflation of desire with the real—that is, the belief that it is parts of the body, the 'literal' penis, the 'literal' vagina, which cause pleasure and desire—is precisely the kind of literalizing fantasy characteristic of the syndrome of melancholic heterosexuality."

JANE
(to Dr. Sigmund)

Sounds like a bad case of *Gender Trouble*.

DR. SIGMUND
(thoughtfully, to Jane)

Well, we're probably hearing a lot of repressed sexual material from the textual unconscious, but we'll need many more sessions to understand it. Some of this stuff that's coming out is pretty bizarre. I mean why in the world would you associate pubic hair with a Coke can?

The Perils of the Text

<u>EXT</u>. THE SMALL BOONDOCK TERMINAL, *which is mobbed by journalists and cameramen*

In one corner, Gilbert, Gubar, and Hirsch are surrounded by a phalanx of shouting REPORTERS.

REPORTER 1
What's your response to this crisis?

REPORTER 2
Do you agree with Allan Bloom? When he made his announcement on TV, he said the text in trouble was Plato's *Symposium.* He's already on the scene with his Syntopicon.

REPORTER 3
Bennett and Cheney claim it's likely to be on their list of endangered books produced by Great Souls. Any comment?

HIRSCH
It doesn't much matter to me what the mystery text is. We only need to know something about it, in case it's part of the cultural heritage literate Americans ought to share. I don't care about Bennett's list. I'm just afraid this one may have escaped from *my* list.

REPORTER 2
Another list of Great Books? Or is this whole thing just a ProfScam?

HIRSCH
"Very few specific titles appear on [my] list, and they usually appear as words not works."
    (*He begins intoning words from his list.*)
"Coolie; cool your heels; Cooper, James Fenimore;

coordination; Copenhagen; Copernicus; copulation; copyright . . . large intestine; La Scala; laser; last laugh, the; Last of the Mohicans, The (title); last shall be first, The; last straw, the; Last Supper, the; Las Vegas . . ." Whether that text out there on the fast track is "Cooper" or "cool your heels," "last straw, the" or "Last Supper, the," I'm here to help save it so that American students everywhere can do better on their College Boards.

The reporters turn to Gilbert and Gubar, but before the collaborators can begin to speak another commuter plane lands, and a new group of passengers enters the terminal: Professors GERALD GRAFF, of Northwestern University; RICHARD OHMANN, of Wesleyan University; HOUSTON BAKER, JR., of the University of Pennsylvania; and LILLIAN S. ROBINSON, an independent scholar. They have journeyed together from Chicago, where all were participants in a conference on "Race, Class, Gender, and Pedagogy." The journalists immediately surround them with flashbulbs popping and microphones at the ready.

REPORTER 1
(pointing a mike at Baker)
Can you confirm that you think it's either a hoagie or a pizza?

REPORTER 2
You've been quoted as saying that choosing between Virginia Woolf and Pearl Buck is "no different from choosing between a hoagie and a pizza."

BAKER
(shielding his eyes against the glare of flashbulbs)
You guys are always misrepresenting everything we say. I never mentioned Woolf or Buck. I only meant to indicate that different texts need to be judged by

different standards. Some people like hoagies, some like pizzas.

REPORTER 1

Well, what is that text out there? Is it "last word, the," Plato's *Symposium,* or a mean graffito?

BAKER

Probably none of those. It might be a novel by Toni Morrison, it might be the blues—*all* the blues. In other words, a product of "the African Body" exploited and assaulted by a racist culture. I'm here to perform "a bold critical act designed to break the interpretive monopoly on Afro-American expressive culture that [has] been held from time immemorial by a white liberal-critical establishment that [sets] 'a single standard of criticism.' "

OHMANN

(to reporters, as he catches sight of Hirsch across the crowded terminal)

I suppose Don Hirsch has been whipping you into a frenzy about cultural literacy. But "researchers [have] found no solid evidence of a decline in reading ability. . . . We are, as so often, experiencing a media-created event."

REPORTER 2

You mean you think there's no text out there? What if it's there and it's by Plato, Milton, Goldsmith?

OHMANN

(musingly)

"Has a good dose of Milton or Goldsmith generally made the farm youth or the Italian immigrant or the recent black arrival in Chicago feel part of a common culture?"

REPORTER 1
Yes, but is there or isn't there a text out there?

ROBINSON
(*interrupting*)
Okay, I'll bet you anything there *is* a text out there, but if it's a text that's been protected for centuries for the wrong reasons, I'm not here to save it, I'm here to commit treason.

Reporters gasp and murmur; some run for the telephone; lightbulbs flash.

ROBINSON
(*continuing firmly*)
All these people who are here to save that text may just want to reinstate an oppressive canon and curriculum. I say there should *be* no hegemonic, male-dominated canon. We shouldn't even save female-authored texts for the wrong reasons. Not if saving one text means excluding another on an arbitrary, elitist basis.

GRAFF
(*to confused reporters, amid general uproar*)
Everything that's happening here just goes to show that "what has proved disabling is not the failure of humanists to *agree* on objectives, but their failure to *disagree* on them in ways which might become recognizable and intelligible to outsiders." If *all* the people here in Boondock would only talk to each other more clearly we could make "ideological conflict into part of what literary study is about." My "conflict model" of education, you know.

The Perils of the Text

EXT. MIDNIGHT, THE FAST TRACK OUTSIDE BOONDOCK

Huge overhead floodlights have been set up to illuminate the scene of the crime. In the distance, on the off-ramp of the bypass, several ambulances and firetrucks are waiting, with engines revved. Gathered around Jane and the trapped Text is a circle of variegated humanists, looking oddly like the diverse crowds of characters one sees in a Fellini movie: a number of bearded men in tweeds, younger ones with punk haircuts and black leather jackets; a woman in a skirt made out of men's ties, another in an elegant sari, still others in jeans or dress-for-success suits; William Bennett with his sleeves rolled up, Stanley Fish and Allan Bloom smoking cigars. Behind them, there is a ring of reporters and photographers, some with videocameras. Behind the journalists, there is a scattering of rubberneckers—including Jennifer, Scott, Officer Friendly, Ghostwriter 1, and the basketball player—most of whom look utterly bewildered. Behind the rubberneckers, Skinheads 1, 2, and 3 are furtively and fumblingly trying to set fire to a cross. All the humanists are shouting except Jane, who is sobbing quietly, as is the Text. In the midst of this, a taxi pulls up and a latecomer, Professor ELIZABETH FOX-GENOVESE, a historian from Emory, emerges and stands quietly just outside the circle.

BENNETT
(yelling at the Text)

I assure you, I have the immense resources of the United States government at my command, but I must know who you are before I deploy them. Just answer a simple question. *Are* you Plato's *Symposium* or are you not?

SCHOLES
(intervening mildly)

You don't have to answer that question. You have a right to be yourself. You don't have to be a "sacred text." You have a right to consult a semiotician.

ACT I

HIRSCH

You *do* have to answer but it's okay if you're the *Symposium*. Just let us know if you're "copyright" or "copulation," "last straw, the" or "Last Supper, the." We'll alphabetize you, and you'll feel a lot better.

BAKER

Tell us if you're the blues, man. We're here to help.

CULLER

(*catching sight of Phyllis Franklin in the crowd*)
I didn't realize you were here. I just wrote you a memo. Isn't this a particularly resonant "text-like situation"? Doesn't it illustrate the "expansion of the domain in which critics work" today?

FRANKLIN

I wouldn't miss it for a Small World or a large one! This is the conference of my dreams!

LENTRICCHIA

(*in an undertone to the Text*)
Who did this to you? Was it Bennett and his thought police trying to maintain their essentialist elitist hegemony in an effort to perpetuate their pernicious colonization of culture?
(*He tears off his jacket, rolls up his sleeves and squares off at Bennett.*)
I'll take that bastard out for you!

BENNETT

(*also squaring off*)
I heard that. Why you "tendentious, ideological" swine, I know *you* did it, you and your radical, subversive, anti-American pals. You did it to compensate for your "loss of nerve and faith" in the sixties.

GRAFF
(*sadly*)
This is an unproductive example of my "conflict model."

ROBINSON
(*aside, to Jane Marple and Jane Tompkins*)
We should get these men out of here. Their stupid macho behavior isn't going to help anything.

Overhearing, Gilbert and Gubar nod sagely.

SG1
It's an obvious case of—

SG2
male anxiety. They're compensating for—

SG1
their own loss of nerve and—

SG2
faith.

ROBINSON
We should only really struggle to reclaim this text if it was composed by "the previously inarticulate, the semi-literate, the consumer of popular literature."

FOX-GENOVESE
(*stepping forward and addressing Robinson*)
I can't agree with you there. "The 'radical' critics of the purportedly irrelevant canon have sacrificed the ideal of collective identity that constituted its most laudable feature. To settle for education as personal autobiography or identity is tacitly to accept the worst forms of

political domination." Anyway, if in your teaching "you do not include a heavy dose of the history of elite males, how do you explain why women and members of minorities are not running the world?"

BENNETT
You talk like "a handmaiden of ideology." I'll get *you*, too!

FOX-GENOVESE
(ignoring him and still addressing Robinson)
I'm just trying to point out that "unless we agree that there is a place for some canon, the apparent issue of whether or not to introduce gender, race, and class is no issue at all. Let me offer you a paradox: It may well be those who reject the narrowness of the established canon, but who remain committed to the validity of some canon . . . who are the true custodians of liberal education or of the humanities."

SCHOLES
(protesting in a courtly manner)
But you know, my dear, that *any* book list imposed arbitrarily and autocratically upon students will result in nothing but superficiality, "trivial knowledge," as well as political conformity to some kind of conservative definition of national identity.

FOX-GENOVESE
Your spirit is "touching," Bob, but your "politics are misguided. Mr. Bennett is, in this respect, correct. The status of the canon is of large political significance. . . . The unpleasant implications of Mr. Bennett's proposals lie not in his attempt to shore up the canon, but in his related—and thinly veiled—determination to re-

verse [the] expansion [of] and restrict access to higher education."

JANE
(*rising to the occasion and looking around keenly*)
You've helped me a lot, Professor Fox-Genovese. Now I know what to do.
(*She turns to the Text.*)
I'm not going to interrogate you any more for the moment; and I'm not going to let these others interrogate you either right now. I'm just going to *read* you.

TEXT
I'd love you to do that!

JANE
Maybe if I just read you carefully enough I can get you off this fast track. In your way, you've been telling me to do that all along. You knew you had an author; you knew there was a material condition inscribed in you; you thought you had readers. As my aunt Jane once told someone, "It ['s] reality you ['re] in touch with and not . . . illusion. You are never deceived by illusion like most of us are. [Now] I realize that, I [see] that I must go by what *you* [think and feel.]"

There is a general murmur of surprise and discontent; a chorus of voices protests.

LENTRICCHIA
Jesus! Agatha Christie as literary theorist?

BENNETT
Worse than that. A Miss Jane Marple mystery as literature!

ACT I

LENTRICCHIA
(*contemptuously to Jane*)
Don't be naive. No act of reading is innocent.

BENNETT
Get away from that text, young woman! It might be dangerous. We still don't know what it is and where it came from.

JANE
I'm going to find out. I'm going to start reading right now. And I'm going to ask some students to help me.
(*She motions to Scott and Jennifer.*)
Come here, you guys. We've got to start reading this minute, and we don't have a lot of time!

The camera PULLS BACK to show Scott and Jennifer timidly moving toward the center of the circle. At the same moment, however, the sound of a train whistle is heard in the distance.

INT. ALISTAIR COOKE'S LIVING ROOM SET

The hosts of the show are seated, with the usual baroque music swelling in the background.

HOST 1
We hope you've enjoyed "The Perils of the Text," this week's installment of "Masterpiece Theatre: An Academic Melodrama." We've tried to introduce you, tonight, to a range of characters representing many points of view current in the wonderful world of the humanities. Of course, any docudrama has to be selective in its depiction of historical crises and changing climates of opinion. Because we wanted to focus on the American way of academic life, we've had to leave out a number of fascinating personalities from the

other side of the Atlantic—especially from Paris and Oxford—who will surely be featured in other shows.

HOST 2

But for now, our questions are obvious. Will Jane succeed in reading the text and will her reading free it from the fast track? Will Scott and Jennifer help her or hinder her? Will the Ghostwriters or the Skinheads triumph in their murderous missions? What about the visiting humanists? Is Lentricchia right to deride Jane as naive? Will he and Bennett come to blows? Which list, if any, will prevail—Allan Bloom's Syntopicon or E. D. Hirsch's *Dictionary of Cultural Literacy?* Will all the feminists—Robinson, Fox-Genovese, Tompkins, and Gilbert and Gubar—ever see eye to eye? Will Graff's "conflict model" or Scholes's semiotics win the day? We're sure you'll want to find out. So here are some highlights from next week's episode.

CUT TO A PENTHOUSE OFFICE IN HOUSTON, TEXAS, THE FOLLOWING MORNING

A high-placed EXXON OFFICIAL is sipping coffee and shouting into a telephone.

OFFICIAL

Goddamn it, I just saw it on "Good Morning, America." Some stupid text is tied to a fast track outside Boondock, Indiana, completely blocking the crossing. There's an idiotic woman reading it out there with a bunch of crazy humanists standing around quarreling. All rail traffic has been stopped in both directions.
(*pauses and sips*)
You're damn right we can't have that. Get your people on the ball.
(*pauses again*)

ACT I

No, it doesn't matter what the damn text is. We've got to clear the area at any cost. Our trainful of maritime supplies has to get through to Alaska. The *Valdez* sails at noon.

CUT BACK TO THE SET OF MASTERPIECE THEATRE

The hosts of show are seated, with the usual baroque music swelling in the background.

HOST 1

Tonight's episode of *Masterpiece Theatre* has been brought to you with assistance from Multijargon Theory, Incorporated, whose researchers ceaselessly labor to test the ideological contents of the sign-systems you encounter in your daily life, and whose motto is "If you're thinking *anything,* you're thinking *something.*"

HOST 2

We are also grateful for aid from Megadose Cultural Vitamins, Limited, whose scientists recommend a Great Book a day to keep the radicals away, and whose motto is "Plato in the service of a kinder, gentler nation."

ACT II

*F*oreign *I*ntrigues; or, *A*bjection on the *E*urocentric *E*xpress

<u>INT</u>. ALISTAIR COOKE'S LIVING ROOM SET
Hosts are seated on either side of a huge TV screen.

HOST 1
Good evening. Welcome to television's one and only *Masterpiece Theatre*. With Alistair Cooke off on assignment in Baghdad, we're once again sitting in for him as hosts of the show, and this time we'll offer you the second installment of our gripping *meta*docudrama, the unprecedented *Masterpiece Theatre* production entitled "Masterpiece Theatre."

HOST 2
Tonight our heroine, Jane Marple, assistant professor of English at Boondock State University, will be swept up in "Foreign Intrigues" as she tries to save the amnesiac Text that has been targeted for extinction by a mysterious assassin.

HOST 1
As you'll remember, at the exciting climax of our last episode, a mass of humanists met outside Boondock and had almost come to blows when a train whistle was heard in the distance: the Exxon company was

ACT II

bringing a load of maritime supplies through to Alaska, in preparation for the sailing of the *Valdez.*

HOST 2
When tonight's episode begins, Jane and the Text are winging their way from the new to the old world.

SOUND OVER: *whine of jet engines, gradually getting louder.*

But let us remind you again that all the situations they'll encounter are fictive and remember, too, that none of our characters should be confused with any "actual" persons, whether those persons experience their subject positions as authentic or playfully mimetic.

EXT. O'HARE AIRPORT

A BOAC 747 is taking off, engines screaming.

INT. THE FIRST-CLASS CABIN

Jane is seated in D1 by the window, and the Text, wrapped in clear plastic, is disguised as a copy of Self *magazine.*

JANE
(*to Text*)
I can't believe that those creeps from Exxon actually sent you to B. Dalton to be remaindered.
(*She closes her eyes wearily.*)

FLASHBACK TO THE FAST TRACK OUTSIDE BOONDOCK

Chaos reigns as a group of RAILROAD OFFICIALS and EXXON FUNCTIONARIES, backed up by a platoon of rifle-wielding state troopers, confront the already embattled humanists who surround Jane, Scott, Jennifer, and the trapped Text.

RAILROAD OFFICIAL
(*to Jane, Scott, Jennifer, and the Text*)
I must inform you that you are trespassing on private property and illegally obstructing our right of way.

EXXON FUNCTIONARY 1
Furthermore, in so doing, you are preventing our corporation from carrying on its internationally urgent business of meeting worldwide needs for regular and super unleaded—or indeed leaded—gasoline, as well as diesel fuel.

EXXON FUNCTIONARY 2
In fact, if you do not clear these tracks at once, our greedy Arab competitors may gain control of our vital market interests, forcing us to mount a costly and time-consuming counterattack on their resources, possibly even an Operation Desert Shield.

PAN TO *a shot of the crowd of humanists surging forward and murmuring* "Rhubarb, rhubarb."

BENNETT
(*interposing himself between the small group around the Text and the large group of officials*)
Speaking for the United States government, stay away from that Text!

OHMANN and GRAFF
(*sardonically, in chorus*)
A dangling modifier from the former head of the NEH!

ACT II

EXXON FUNCTIONARY 2
(in an undertone to Bennett)

Don't forget our international priorities. Which is more important, some dumb text or getting supplies to the Contras?

LENTRICCHIA
(to Jameson)

This perfect instance of institutionalized corporate violence will make an excellent starting point for a problematization of the rhetoric of oil.

JAMESON

Crude but crucial. Perhaps we should found a center for Critical Energy Science Studies?

ALLAN BLOOM

Ah, yes. CESS as in "Cesspool."

BENNETT
(to Exxon functionaries)

Of course, when it comes to American interests abroad, I'm no dope, but what if this text is one of the pillars of our free-market economy—the Constitution, the Yellow Rose of Texas, the *Wall Street Journal!*

EXXON FUNCTIONARY 1
(suavely)

If so, you know as well as I do, sir, that the free market always takes care of its own.
(He motions to the state troopers, who disentangle the Text from the tracks and begin hustling it toward a nearby Black Maria.)
This text can only gain from enlightened arbitrage by a qualified literary broker. You can be sure we'll put it

in good hands. We won't hurt a single one of its dots or dashes.

BENNETT
(*brightening*)
Perhaps its value *should* be determined by the market-place.

TEXT
(*screaming to Jane, as it is being dragged into the Black Maria*)
Help me, help me. They're going to rub me out!

JANE
(*screaming back, although she is being restrained by two burly state troopers*)
Don't worry. Wherever they take you, I'll track you down. I'll save you and I'll read you yet!

CUT BACK TO *Jane and the Text on the airplane*

TEXT
(*shuddering*)
It was so humiliating lying on that table in the B. Dalton on Lexington Avenue. They priced me at ninety-nine cents and then marked me down. There was a 1987 Persian Cat calendar right next to me and that got bought first!

JANE
At least they didn't recycle you. But the people at Exxon would never think of recycling, would they?

TEXT
They were ruthless, ruthless. They had no respect for me as a linguistic construct. They just dumped me in

that bookstore, saying that if I was worth anything, somebody would buy me, but nobody seemed to care about me one bit.

JANE
(*sympathetically*)

You weren't even properly commodified. It's a lucky thing, after all, that my old friend from graduate school never did get a teaching job. Why, if he hadn't ended up working in the mail room at Exxon's New York office, I might never have found you!

TEXT
(*flirtatiously*)

Well, anyway, you and those two nice men over there projected meaning into me. And made me into an object of exchange.

JANE
(*eagerly*)

It was as if we were destined to meet again. I still want to read you, you know.

TEXT

I know you do, but the plot line here is indeterminate. Why are we here?

JANE

Don't you realize that you've moved from the margin to the center. Roger Kimball, author of *Tenured Radicals: How Politics Has Corrupted Our Higher Education,* and Charles J. Sykes, author of *ProfScam: Professors and the Demise of Higher Education,* bought you at B. Dalton one minute before I arrived from Boondock, Indiana. They think you're a monument of unaging intellect. There they are over there. They're taking us both to

England, where a really serious scholar, at Oxford or Cambridge, might be able to identify you.

TEXT

Do you mean they're not against interpretation in England? They might be able to say something determinate about my signifiers?

JANE

Shhhh. Here comes the flight attendant. Remember that you're disguised as *Self* magazine. Talk like *Self!*

FLIGHT ATTENDANT

Hi, I'm Stacey. I'll be taking care of you tonight on your flight to Heathrow. And you're—?

JANE

Jane Marple.

TEXT
(becoming table of contents from Self *magazine)*
I'm Okay, You're Not.

STACEY

What'll you be having for dinner, Jane?

TEXT
(as Self*)*
Never Eat Standing Up.

JANE

I'll have the chateaubriand, thanks, Stacey.

STACEY

And, like, with the meal?

ACT II

                    TEXT
                  (*as* Self)
Undressing for Success.

                    JANE
A glass of white wine, please.

                    TEXT
                  (*as* Self)
Sex at Your Computer.

                   STACEY
I see you're reading, like, *Self,* one of my favorite mags.

                    TEXT
                  (*as* Self)
How to Love Your Own Thighs.

                    JANE
          (*suddenly breaking down and weeping*)
No, no, that's not a real magazine. It's an indeterminate text that's been somehow abandoned, kind of like
a missing person. I'm just trying to help it!

                    TEXT
                  (*as* Self)
His and Her Facials: How Safe Are Cosmetics?

                    JANE
Two journalists are trying to help us. There they are,
one row forward, Sykes and Kimball. But who is that
strange man with them? He looks vaguely familiar.

                   STACEY
Let me get you a drink.

TEXT
(*stammering in confusion*)
Men Who Hate Women and the Women Who Hate—
no, **Men Who Love Women and the Women Who
Despise Them**—no, **Women Who ... Men Who ...**

JANE
Can't you stop yourself? You're getting yourself mixed
up with your cover.

PAN TO one row forward, *where a SILVERY-HAIRED MAN un-
buckles his seat belt, rises, and moves toward Jane and the Text.*

JANE
Oh, I *do* know you.

SILVERY-HAIRED MAN
Good evening, welcome to *Masterpiece Theatre*.

JANE
You're, you're—Alistair Cooke!

COOKE
Yes, and you and your friend over here are the next
episode of my program.

JANE
You mean, right now—? Postmodernism? A meta-
moment?

COOKE
If you thought we at Mobil would let Exxon get away
with you and your text, you were very much mistaken.

ACT II

TEXT
(*as* Self, *pathetically*)
As the World Earns: How to Profit from Global Investing.

JANE
But Kimball and Sykes said they'd lead us out of "the weird world of the academic journals," the "crucifixion of teaching," and "the new sophistry."

COOKE
My dear lady, Kimball and Sykes are my operatives. When I heard about the plight of your text, I realized at once that it was most likely *The Proud and the Prejudiced,* our lost televersion of Jane Austen's great novel. Mobil is turning you over to the BBC for your own good. Americans don't know how to package masterpieces properly.

TEXT
(*as* Self, *whimpering*)
A Handbook for Shopaholics.

JANE
(*to the Text*)
It's no use. He knows you're not *Self.*

TEXT
How can *he* know if I'm not sure myself?

JANE
I don't understand either. Why he hasn't even examined any of your cruxes, not to mention your signifiers. I don't think we can trust the validity of his interpretation.

CUT TO *KIMBALL and SYKES, who are drinking champagne across the aisle.*

SYKES
I'm glad we could liberate that text from the "obscurantists, sorcerers, and witch doctors of profthink."

KIMBALL
I'm sure there'll be room for both our books about this latest academic scandal. "Liberalism's belief in meritocracy is being overwhelmed by a variety of florid radicalisms, all of which congregate under the term multiculturalism. . . . That is intellectual tyranny."

SYKES
I don't know about you or your *Tenured Radicals,* but I got a better advance for this one than I did for *ProfScam.*

CUT BACK TO *Jane, trying to comfort the Text, as Stacey appears with a bottle of Chardonnay.*

STACEY
Here's some wine. And, like, I figured it out.
(*She turns to Text.*)
I know who you are. You're a novel that somebody left behind on this plane yesterday! I saw you sliding around in the overhead compartment. You're *Pet Sematary* by Stephen King.

COOKE
(*disregarding her and reassuring the Text*)
Don't worry. You'll feel a lot better once we get you back on the telly, where you belong.

ACT II

He starts up the aisle to his own seat. Jane's gaze and the camera follow him but are suddenly transfixed by a peculiar couple in row B: dressed in soiled workclothes, smudged with what looks like coaldust, and carrying a metal lunch pail, the man appears to be a miner, although he is wearing wire-rimmed glasses and reading a copy of The 18th Brumaire; *stranger still, his companion looks like a Scandinavian model, although she is leafing through a copy of* Pouvoir d'Horreur *by Julia Kristeva.*

CUT BACK TO *Jane, who is frowning as she sips her Chardonnay.*

JANE
Am I getting paranoid? Or do *they* look familiar too?

INT. THE NEXT DAY, LUNCHTIME, THE BAR OF THE MUSEUM TAVERN, ACROSS THE ROAD FROM THE BRITISH MUSEUM

Two eminent transatlantic critics—GEORGE STEINER and DENIS DONOGHUE—are downing pints of Guinness and nibbling Scotch eggs with ROBERT ALTER of the University of California, Berkeley, and Harold Bloom of Yale and New York universities, who have just arrived in London for an international conference of Bible scholars.

STEINER
(gloomily)
Americanization is of course destroying culture. No doubt that is why that neurotic young American woman so rashly abducted an upcoming episode of *Masterpiece Theatre* this morning. Did you see the story in *The Independent?* I suppose she thinks she's made away with *The Color Purple* or one of those other works of "the most derivative or passing interest" that are so popular with intellectuals in the States.

DONOGHUE
(*with equal gloom*)
Some of those people would actually have us "believe that literary criteria are incorrigibly man-made values."

STEINER
(*ignoring him*)
Imagine, at Harvard, the "bellwether of American universities," someone even offers "a course on black women novelists of the early 1980s."

BLOOM
(*taking umbrage*)
But of course, my dear, there are women writers and women writers. There is, after all, as I am myself about to reveal, the strongest author of them all, the author-*ess* of the Book of J.

ALTER
(*scornfully*)
Not J, it's R who is the strongest of them all.
(*emphatically*)
He, R, put together the texts of J, E, D, and P.

BLOOM
(*staring off into space and ignoring him*)
By J, I have it. That young woman who just absconded with the Text this morning. She doesn't think it's *The Color Purple*, she knows it's *The Book of J* and she wants to use it, or shall I say *abuse* it, in a Women's Studies course! Just what I'd expect from one of these ideological mediocrities.
(*scowls and spits*)
Marxists, feminists, New Historicists, members of a "school of resentment," acolytes of "Foucault with soda water," an entire "rabblement of lemmings."

ACT II

CUT TO *the other end of the bar where Jane, wearing sunglasses and a raincoat, is hunched over a Coca Cola, studying the Text, which is disguised as one of Rupert Murdoch's dailies.*

JANE
(to Text)
Well at least we know you're not the Elgin Marbles, so our trip to the BM was not for nil.

TEXT
INSIDE SCOOP! SECRET PIX OF DI AND FERGIE!

JANE
(thoughtfully)
But I'd love to go back to the reading room tomorrow. Maybe a Hinman Collator would help—

TEXT
THATCHER CLOSES POLYS. TELLS PROFS TO SCRAM!

PAN TO *entrance of pub. A coalminer and a Scandinavian model are surveying the smoky crowded room with narrowed eyes.*

JANE
Oh my God, there they are again. Am I confronting the return of the repressed?

TEXT
TEXT-NAP CAPER AT BBC. YANKEE LIBBER SUSPECTED.

PAN BACK TO *Steiner, Alter, Donoghue, and Bloom.*

STEINER
These American universities. Pure naiveté! Everyone knows that "given a free vote, the bulk of humankind will choose football, the soap opera, or bingo over Aes-

chylus. . . . The canon is forged and perpetuated by the few."

ALTER
(*ignoring him and turning crossly to Bloom*)
Your so-called "authoress" of J is just your own personal fiction anyway.

BLOOM
(*proudly*)
My supreme fiction!

ALTER
Which, from your point of view, makes you the author of the authoress of God!

DONOGHUE
(*ignoring both*)
And some of those American anticanon critics. All I can say is that "feminist criticism seems at its present stage to me to be a libel upon women."

STEINER
(*his voice rising in passion*)
"Is there in the almost total absence from drama of any major woman writer some formidable hint? Is the biological capacity for procreation, for engendering formed life which is cardinal to woman, in some way, at some level, absolutely primordial to a woman's being, so creative, so fulfilling, as to subvert, as to render comparatively pallid, the begetting of fictive personae which is the matter of drama and of so much representative art?"

PAN TO *Jane, addressing BARTENDER.*

JANE
Could I please have some more ice for my Coke?

ACT II

BARTENDER
(*in a tone of loud disgust*)
Why bless you, luv, you've got a cube already. This isn't the States, you know.

PAN BACK TO *Steiner, Alter, Donoghue, and Bloom.*

DONOGHUE
(*thoughtfully*)
An American woman.

He, Alter, Bloom, and Steiner stare hard at Jane, as do the miner and the model.

PAN TO *Jane.*

JANE
(*to the Text*)
These people are problematic. We've got to get out of here.

TEXT
(*desperately*)
INSIDE SCOOP: SECRET PIX OF CHARLES AND CAMILLA. INSIDE SCOOP: SECRET PIX OF QUEEN MUM AND MICK JAGGER. IN-SIDE SCOOP: SECRET PIX OF PHILLIP AND POPE.

JANE
That's it. We'll change our disguise. We'll leave London and go to Oxford. I'll get a reading ticket for the Bodleian, where I can read you in peace, and we'll be two characters none of these people would ever care about. I'll be an exchange student—I'll be Jennifer, from Boondock State—and you'll be my term paper for that required lit. course. Can you literalize that?

TEXT

Certainly. I'll just play fast and loose with my signifiers.

JANE

(*dramatically, as Jennifer*)

Awesome. Excellent. I can really relate to that.

TEXT

(*just as dramatically, as final paper*)

Unlike a fontanel, a sonnet consists of a closing couplet following four quadroons. But the "Lake Isle of Industry" by William Yeats shows up poetry during the fantasy eclair. When William wrote it—

JANE/JENNIFER

I mean, like, what I think is that we should really get going now, right?

TEXT

(*as final paper, voice trailing off as Jane hurries toward the door of the bar*)

William saw that things had changed since the uprising of the pheasants against the nobility and since the time when Magellan circumcized the globe in his forty-foot clipper . . .

EXT. WASHINGTON, D.C., THE WHITE HOUSE

GEORGE and BARBARA BUSH are watching a TV special on country music in their private living quarters.

GEORGE

(*munching on a pork crackling*)

If you're going to start with the literacy thing again, Bar, "I will never apologize for the United States of America. I don't care what the facts are."

ACT II

BARBARA

But dear, a text has been stolen and Lynne thinks it might be an important one. Don't you want to—

GEORGE

(*stubbornly*)

When I got to be president I stopped having to eat broccoli, and I don't see why I can't stop having to read texts too!

BARBARA

If you don't care what Lynne thinks, you might worry about what Dick suspects. A hostage crisis, for instance.

GEORGE

(*with a grin that turns into a grimace*)

Now Bar, you know we don't use the H word around here! But "obviously, when you see somebody go berserk and get a weapon and go in and murder people, of course, it troubles me."

BARBARA

(*patting his hand reassuringly*)

And H stands for Helms, too. Jesse might call you un-American or un-Christian. Suppose the text is a prayer or something.

GEORGE

(*glumly*)

The religion thing?

BARBARA

(*briskly*)

Or the literacy thing. *Or* the broccoli thing.

(*She passes him a plate of raw vegetables.*)

Eat some. And don't forget that the NEH is married to the Defense Department!

GEORGE
(*moving closer to the TV*)
"When I need a little free advice about Saddam Hussein, I turn to country music."

<u>INT</u>. THE ADMISSIONS OFFICE OF THE BODLEIAN LIBRARY, OXFORD

Jane/Jennifer, wearing a backpack and carrying the Text, is arguing with a gowned ADMINISTRATOR. Although she doesn't see them, the miner and the model are watching her from a corner of the room.

JANE/JENNIFER
But I've shown you my student ID. What else do I need to get into the library?

ADMINISTRATOR
(*haughtily*)
I'm sorry, madam, but you need a recommender.

JANE/JENNIFER
What's that?

ADMINISTRATOR
One of us, actually.

ZOOM IN on *a corner, where the miner and the model are conferring in an undertone.*

MINER
(*pulling an Oxford gown from his lunchpail, tossing it on, and revealing himself as TERRY EAGLETON, Marxist supercritic*)
No matter what it is, that Text is a crucial discursive system which ought not to be left in the hands of a

young woman who may, after all, inscribe it into a hegemonic order where it will no doubt be nostalgically or regressively defined as "literature."

MODEL
(looking shocked as, pulling on a sweatshirt bearing the motto "Moi C'est Moi?", she reveals herself as TORIL MOI, metapostfeminist metacritic)
Do you mean she might be a naive essentialist? A phallologocrat?

EAGLETON
(with a snarl of contempt)
Just look at the way she's been mooning over that Text. Precisely the sort of "soggy subjectivism" I loathe. It leads to the petit bourgeois fetishizing of the work of art.

MOI
You may be right. Like so many misguided American feminist critics, she probably thinks that the text has "integrity and totality"—"a phallic construct." In fact, since "the phallus is often conceived of as a whole, unitary and simple form," that sort of woman's totalizing and essentializing belief "in unitary wholes plays directly into the hands of . . . phallic aesthetic criteria."

EAGLETON
It's worse than that. Although she doesn't even realize it, she's nothing but a servant of the bourgeois capitalist status quo. Without us, she'll never escape from Alistair Cooke and the minions of Mobil Oil.
(He snorts and glares.)

CUT BACK TO *the administrator's desk. Jane is still desperately arguing her case to the Bodleian admissions officer.*

JANE/JENNIFER
I have my term paper with me. Won't that prove that I'm who I say I am?

TEXT
(*as student paper*)
In William Yeats's choice of styles, he showed that he understood a lot about the hierarchy of genres, which means the man is on top and the woman on the bottom.

ADMINISTRATOR
Madam, I'm afraid that won't do.

EAGLETON
(*stepping forward*)
Might I intervene and offer myself as a recommender?

MOI
(*also stepping forward*)
I too would like to enact an intervention here.
(*in an undertone, to Jane*)
Or even a subversion.

JANE
(*dropping her cover as understanding slowly dawns*)
Why I know who you both are. *Literary Theory, Sexual/ Textual Politics.* I've heard you speak at conferences. But weren't you on the plane too, and in the pub, only dressed differently?

ACT II

EAGLETON
(*smiling benignly*)
We could hardly leave you to the tender mercies of Mr. Cooke. As Timothy Brennan has incisively observed, "*Masterpiece Theatre* is a cultural colonization in the heart of empire." Or, in my own words, "capitalism's reverential hat-tipping to the arts is obvious hypocrisy, except when it can hang them on its walls as a sound investment." That's what Cooke wants to do with you and your friend over here.

JANE
(*slowly*)
Well, I did think there was something suspect about Alistair Cooke showing up when he did.

TEXT
(*frantically continuing to disguise itself as a student paper*)
As for William's famous poem "Leda and the Swan," that was no common bird-woman relationship!

MOI
(*kindly*)
Notice that this Text wishes to reenact phallocratic domination. A scene of rape. It is refusing "revolutionary agency."

JANE
But what if it is an important work of literature, a play by Shakespeare, for example?

EAGLETON
What difference would that make? Why do you insist on believing that "certain pieces of writing" should be "selected as being more amenable" to study "than others"? Such a notion on your part is "the embarrassment of literary criticism," which "defines for itself a special

object." A text—be it a discursive field like a novel or a social event like a party—"can prove quite as rich as one of the canonical works, and critical dissections of it quite as ingenious as those of Shakespeare."

TEXT
(eagerly emerging from its disguise)
A party? Am I the Labor party? The Communist party? A cocktail party?

JANE
(to Text)
I think he was speaking metaphorically.

MOI
(also to Text)
He was meditating, quite rightly, on the relationship between the free play of the signifier and the material conditions governing discourse.

EAGLETON
(also addressing the Text)
But it is possible that you have been produced by "the strongly emergent movement of working-class writing," and, if so, let me propose an allegory to you: "*We* know that the lion is stronger than the lion-tamer, and so does the lion-tamer. The problem is that the lion does not know it. It is not out of the question that the death of literature may help the lion to awaken."

JANE
The death of literature?

MOI
As crucial as the death of the author. "We must take one further step and proclaim with Roland Barthes the death of the author."

ACT II

JANE
The death of the author?

TEXT
(*shivering*)
The death of the Text?

ADMINISTRATOR
(*interrupting*)
Closing time, ladies and gentlemen. Hurry up please.

EAGLETON
(*to Jane*)
Well, then, you'll meet us here tomorrow at nine sharp, won't you? After all, you don't want this text to be "hermetically sealed from history, subjected to a sterile critical formalism, piously swaddled with eternal verities and used to confirm prejudices which any moderately enlightened student can perceive to be objectionable." Its "liberation . . . from such controls may well entail the death of literature, but it may also be [its] redemption." Toril and I are therefore pleased to be your recommenders.
(*aside, to Moi*)
How appropriately ironic that we will free this text from the clutches of a liberal humanist and her false class consciousness in the hallowed space of Duke Humfreys!

MOI
(*ecstatically*)
Yes, as a feminist I have to liberate the text from "patriarchal notions of cultural criticism as a 'value-free' exercise," even (or perhaps especially) if that criticism is espoused by what is ordinarily called a feminist.

CUT TO *the doorway of the admissions office. Moi and Eagleton exit. Behind them, Jane sees another odd couple being turned away by the Bodleian guard: a WOMAN IN A SARI and a MAN WEAR-ING AN ARAB HEADDRESS. She frowns but is interrupted by a plaintive question from the Text.*

TEXT
What was all that about a lion?

JANE
Never mind. I have a plan. We'll leave tomorrow morning on the boat train to Paris. I'll wire my brilliant Uncle Hercule Poirot, who teaches at the Ecole des Hauts Études. I'm sure he can help us. We've got to get out of this lion's den.

<u>INT</u>. THE OFFICE OF SENATOR JESSE HELMS, IN WASHINGTON, D.C.

Helms, red-faced, is pounding on his desk and shouting into the phone.

HELMS
"If America persists in the way it's going, and the Lord doesn't strike us down, he ought to apologize to Sodom and Gomorrah." Oh Lord, find that text and strike it down. It's probably a crucifix dipped in urine or one of those obscene Mapplethorpe photographs or a Planned Parenthood brochure. Strike it down, Lord, strike it down.

He pauses, gnawing on the wooden stem of a small American flag.

ACT II

HELMS

You guys at the FBI have always been the right hand of the Lord. Don't fail Him now. I'm working on a constitutional amendment that will get those immoral northern liberals at the NEA and the NEH. But I need you now. I need you to exterminate the brutes. Or, as Pat Robertson's Christian Coalition points out, those liberals will "use their money [and that text] to teach [our] sons how to sodomize one another."

He pauses again, wrapping the flag around his little finger.

HELMS

George is a wimp. Everybody knows that. A nerd. But I've got a list. Get this and get this for sure. Target that text and target those homosexuals, abortionists, pacifists, and perverts who probably wrote it. I mean, we're living in an America where Martin Luther King has a holiday named after him and *The Last Temptation of Christ* was shown on Easter Sunday at Boondock State. Here's my list of culprits, just for now: "Audre Lorde, Minnie Bruce Pratt, Christos, Annie Sprinkle, and David Wojnarowisz," as well as the San Francisco Lesbian and Gay Film Festival. Get them. Get them all. And get that missing text. Seeing and reading are dangerous. Make that text invisible, Lord. It's better dead than read.

INT. THE BOAT TRAIN TO PARIS

Jane and the Text, still disguised as Jennifer and her final lit. paper, are spending the night in a second-class compartment. Opposite them, are the woman in the sari and the man wearing an Arab headdress. Both look considerably more westernized than they did earlier. The woman has a punk hairdo and is leafing restlessly through a copy of Elle *magazine, while the man is listening to a*

82

Walkman, the cord of which dangles from under his headdress; tinny sounds of Glenn Gould playing Liszt's transcription of Beethoven's Fifth Symphony can be vaguely heard.

TEXT
(as student paper)

When in William's great poem "Sailing to Byzantium," he decided to become a golden bird, his sense of self was greatly altered.

JANE/JENNIFER
(loudly)

I think you're really really awesome. And how could I have written you? It's only because the library is such a wonderful suppository of knowledge.

(in an undertone, to the Text.)

I don't feel a bit guilty about standing up Eagleton and Moi, and I hope you don't either. They were probably out to get you—and anyway, who's to say that they even exist? They themselves don't think that they're the transcendental signifiers of their own texts.

TEXT
(as final paper)

Unlike Keats, at this point in time Yeats had no theory of negative culpability.

WOMAN IN SARI
(studying a photostory of Christian LaCroix's summer collection)

I can't help noticing that you are engaged in an exercise in allegorizing the subject position of William Butler Yeats. I too have attempted such a performance. But "even if one honed a critical methodology sensitive and vulnerable to this understanding, there would remain the articulated specificity of the 'somethings' that the text wishes, on one level, to mean, and with which it ruses."

JANE
(*in a whisper, to the Text*)
She may be on to you. She seems to think you're a ruse.

WOMAN IN SARI
Ah those "somethings," ah those ruses. "Within a shifting and abyssal frame, these . . . are the 'material' to which we as readers, with our own elusive historico-politico-economico-sexual determinations, bring the machinery of our reading and our judgment."

MAN IN HEADRESS
(*turning down his Walkman and nodding in agreement*)
"The effects of writing can be grave indeed." And of course "any centrist, exclusivist conception of the text . . . ignores the self-confirming will to power from which many texts can spring."

JANE
(*to Text*)
O dear; she thinks you may be a ruse, and he thinks you may spring from a will to power.

TEXT
(*even more desperately babbling as student paper*)
I will also study two important ideas that appear in the poetry of William Yeats: the lamination of Christ and the denunciation of the Virgin.

JANE/JENNIFER
(*frightened and politely trying to leave*)
Is my essay freaking you? Maybe I should just take it to another part of the train.

MAN IN HEADRESS
(*smoothly*)
Please don't leave, Professor Marple. We know who
you are and we think we know what your text is. Allow
me to introduce myself and my colleague. I am Edward
Said of Columbia University, and my associate here is
Gayatri Chakravorty Spivak of the University of Pittsburgh. We believe your text to inscribe the unheard
and untold sufferings of the colonized. In short, we
believe yours is a subaltern text.

SPIVAK
(*musing over an ad for Ralph Lauren's* Safari)
"The crosshatching of the revolutionary nonpossessive
possibilities in the structure of writing in general and
its control by subaltern phonocentrism gives us access
to the micrology . . . of the subaltern's philosophical
world."

SAID
Your text, Professor Marple, was of course tied up on
that railroad track outside Boondock because the subaltern text is always "maliciously portrayed and essen-
tialized" in the West.

JANE
But, after all, Alistair Cooke wanted to put this text on
Masterpiece Theatre, didn't he?

SAID
(*laughing bitterly*)
A likely story. "The colonial encounter continues."
The great oil companies have always coopted cultural
alterity. Alistair Cooke obviously wanted to brainwash
your text and make it into an imperialist zombie!

ACT II

JANE

(*slowly, thinking aloud, and abandoning her disguise as Jennifer*)

Well, he was disturbing. But I thought Eagleton and Moi were pretty problematic too. They seemed to be looking forward to the death of literature! And this text might *be* literature!

SPIVAK

I can sympathize with Moi, at least. "What . . . must a woman do with the reactionary sexual ideology of high art? . . . Must one simply honor the breach between 'the field of action' and the 'field of art' and function by means of an ever-abreactive historical analysis?"

(*She begins turning the pages of a Banana Republic catalog.*)

In my future work I will put it this way: "How can ontology lay hold of a fart?"

JANE

That's a good question, I guess.

TEXT

(*plaintively*)

My signifiers are beginning to ache.

SAID

(*turning up his Walkman so that "The Ride of the Valkyrie" is heard quite distinctly*)

"Empire as a way of life," a telling phrase . . . "a culture . . . with a whole history of exterminism and incorporation behind it."

JANE

(*turning ingratiatingly to Spivak*)

I know your French is good. Maybe you can help me. I'm trying to find my Uncle Hercule, who teaches at the Ecole des Hauts Études, but I don't know much about Paris at all.

SPIVAK
(*coyly*)
Well, you might say that, "situated [as I am] within the current academic theater of cultural imperialism" I have a "certain *carte d'entrée* into the elite theoretical *ateliers* in Paris." I'll be glad to guide you and provide you with both *parole* and *langue,* as necessary.

As the train glides into the Gare du Nord, Jane rises to exit, carrying the Text, but Spivak and Said linger a moment.

SAID
(*to Spivak*)
I hope you noticed her totalizing discourse. She is no doubt part of a "strident chorus of rightward-tending damnation in which what is nonwhite, non-Western, and non–Judeo-Christian is herded together under the rubric of terrorism and/or evil." We must liberate that oppressed text from her imperialist clutches!

SPIVAK
(*enthusiastically*)
And that text might represent what I have called the "discourse of the clitoris." "Even as I acknowledge and honor its irreducible physiological effect," I must tease it out of its "reduction to a physiological fantasy."

EXT. THE CORNER OF FORTY-SECOND STREET AND BROADWAY

A trench-coated DAN RATHER is surrounded by an eager crowd, many of whom are waving excitedly at the video cameras stationed around him.

ACT II

RATHER
(looking intently into camera)
I'm on location here at Times Square with a group of ordinary Americans, all fired up about the missing text. Let's get their opinions.
(He thrusts a microphone into the crowd.)
You, sir. What's your view?

MAN IN SWEATS WITH SUNGLASSES
(shouting)
It's Michael Jackson's new Pepsi commercial. Absolutely. A national disgrace. That woman wants to sell it to the Japanese.

WOMAN IN CURLERS
(elbowing her way in front of him)
That's stupid. It's Elvis's last words. He appeared to me in a dream last night looking very sad.

WOMAN IN BLACK
(carrying religious leaflets)
God forgive you, you're both wrong.
(She falls onto her knees, crossing herself.)
It's the tortilla with the face of our Lord Jesus upon it. Stolen by godless followers of Satan.

RATHER
(appearing nervous and buttonholing a man in a business suit)
You, sir. What's your opinion?

MAN IN BUSINESS SUIT
A tax-free municipal, a T-bill. That's what those foreigners are trying to get their hands on. They always—

A harried-looking, prematurely aged man interrupts.

HARRIED MAN

Nonsense. As a high school teacher, I can speak with some authority. Unfortunately, that lost text is our slow learners' version of *Billy Budd*, written in words of one syllable or less for remedial classes. We had only one copy for two thousand seniors and we haven't been able to locate it in weeks.

RAPPERS appear, knocking him down and jeering.

RAPPERS

Why you want to save that Text?
We say hex
To that Text!
We the future,
We the next.
Lick *our* Text up and down—
Lick it till your tongue turns doo-doo brown.

RATHER
(*backing away and speaking into his mike*)
Well, that about wraps it up here in the Big Apple. As you can see, feelings are running high and—

Around him, the crowd explodes into incoherent slogans.

VOICE 1

The Madonna of the spaghetti billboard!

VOICE 2

Tide was Designed, With Mothers in Mind, To Get out the Dirt Kids Get Into.

VOICE 3

The unexpurgated *Snow White!*

ACT II

VOICE 4
A Primer of Safe Sex for Pre-Teens!

VOICE 5
Men Who Hate Women and the Women Who Love Them!

VOICE 6
Tammy Fay Bakker's Make-Up Secrets!

FADE OUT

<u>INT</u>. A TWA L1011

Professors Sandra Gilbert and Susan Gubar, frequent flyers, are watching the sun rise over the coast of Ireland.

SG1
These jokes are just going to make us look like snobbish elitists or like liberal humanists—and if we're thought to take pride in being human, the next thing you know they'll accuse us of being "speciesists."

SG2
Speciesism: Discrimination against or exploitation of certain animal species, based on the assumption of mankind's superiority.

SG1
So. Do you really want to put on airs about not being an animal?

FLIGHT ATTENDANT
(*pausing as she passes up the aisle*)
Hi, remember me, I'm Tracey. My friend Stacey wanted to know whether you were missing a book by Stephen King called *Pet Sematary*.

<u>INT</u>. A TABLE AT THE DEUX MAGOTS, IN THE SIXTH ARONDISSEMENT

Jane, Said, Spivak, and the Text are drinking kirs *with Jane's uncle, HERCULE POIROT, who is flanked by the French philosopher JACQUES DERRIDA and GEOFFREY HARTMAN of Yale University.*

POIROT
(to the Text)
Calm yourself, I beg you. Me, I am of the most competent
(twirls his mustache)
—as your friend here must know from her studies of the genre in which I play a part so magnifique—I am the world's greatest detective, formerly head of the Belgian Police Force, and a power to reckon with in Paris, where I lecture often on detection, deconstruction, dissemination, defamiliarization, and deception.

JANE
(awestruck)
Oh Uncle Hercule, I was sure you could—

POIROT
And you, my child, relax yourself also. I assure you that I have my little idea about your Text—my suspicion, shall we say.
(He leans toward Derrida and speaks in an undertone.)
Fear not, cher maître, I will carry out your mission. This text, as you have so incisively argued, will exonerate the evilly maligned memory of our much lamented friend Paul de Man, and I will have no difficulty in stealing it away from my naive American niece.

ACT II

(replying to Poirot, also in an undertone)
If I may speak frankly, indeed if I may speak at all, given that speech must always be severely interrogated, I am of two minds about the identity of this infinitely cryptic, at once opened and closed, folded/ unfolded text. It "veils itself. It remains in a veiled concealment (*Verborgenheit*) which itself veils itself."

He turns to the table at large and speaks loudly in double columns.

Column A

"Let us say, then, 'on the one hand . . . on the other hand,' and what is more 'on the one hand . . . on the other hand' on both hands. On both hands, both sides it would be necessary to pursue further the overdetermining division." "More often than ever before, with the case of what has become a 'case' in the newspapers—the 'de Man case'—I have wondered: What will remain of all this in a few years, in ten years, in twenty years? . . . [Are] these precipitous and compulsive publications [attacking my friend and

Column B

"Woman (truth) will not be pinned down. In truth woman, truth will not be pinned down. That which will not be pinned down by truth is, in truth—*feminine*. . . . The divergence within truth elevates itself. It is elevated in quotation marks. . . . Because woman is (her own) writing, style must return to her. In other words, it could be said that if style were a man (much as the penis according to Freud is the 'normal prototype of fetishes'), then writing would be a woman. But in the midst of all these weapons circulating from hand to hand, passing my defense of my friend] essentially 'biodegradable' because destined to advance to oblivion . . . [?] . . . I am going to stop. I have once again been too verbose and too elliptical. Someone, guess who, is perhaps going to reproach *Critical Inquiry* for publishing me too often and at too great a length. . . . I give notice right now that I am tired of this scene. . . ."

from one opponent to another, the question still remains of what I am about here."

HARTMAN
(benevolently, to Jane)
These "are exercises that the mind performs repeatedly, exhaustingly, beyond the possibility of immediate benefit of an obvious kind."

SPIVAK
(passionately, to Said)
I have myself continually insisted on the crucial role of the feminine. Have I not observed on numerous occasions that "Into the (n)ever-virgin, (n)ever-violated hymen of interpretation . . . is spilled the seed of meaning; a seed that scatters itself abroad rather than inseminates." It's so exciting.

JANE
(blushing, to Spivak and Said)
But I thought that you two thought this was a colonized subaltern text.

ACT II

TEXT
(*muttering discontentedly to itself*)
I feel as if I'm being erased.

POIROT
(*in an undertone to Derrida*)
As you have pointed out, de Man "also gave texts to a resistance publication" and me, I am virtually certain that this text is that very resistance journal, *Exercice du silence,* which will fully vindicate my old Belgian colleague.

DERRIDA
(*losing control and shouting irascibly*)
I admit that my friend de Man wrote—and I am quoting him—"a solution of the Jewish problem that would aim at the creation of a Jewish colony isolated from Europe would not entail, for the literary life of the West, deplorable consequences." But surely he was at least on the other hand producing an "uncompromising critique of 'vulgar anti-Semitism.' "

SAID
The creation of a Jewish colony always already isolated from Europe! A product of "Zionist imperialism. . . . The schematic picture [I have sketched] of organized Zionist power in the United States is, if anything, understated."

HARTMAN
(*with ironic courtesy*)
On the subject of what he is pleased to call "Zionist imperialism," I must always already beg to disagree with my learned colleague.

SAID
(leaping to his feet)

I have no patience with this endless "semantic niggling."

(He turns ferociously on Jane.)

Who is this so-called "Jane Marple" anyway? Is she herself anything more than an imperialist fictional construct, a secret agent of the colonizers? No doubt Jane Marple is actually "Jane Marple," an "ideological simulacrum whose only purpose is to [stop the] irreversible progress [of this text] toward self-determination."

(to Spivak, as he starts toward the door)

Come on, Gayatri, let's get a little help from our developing world friends.

Before Spivak can respond, Jane rises, hissing to the Text.

JANE
(to Text)

I'm afraid each of these people may have a reason to try to deconstruct you.

(to the group)

Will you excuse me and my Text for a moment?

TEXT
(hissing back at Jane)

Who are you anyway? Are you Jane Marple, the way you said you were, or are you "Jane Marple"? And who am I? I feel afraid and frayed and shredded.

JANE

Let's get out of here.

INT. THE LADIES' ROOM OF THE CAFE

The Text is speaking urgently to Jane.

ACT II

TEXT

What's wrong with me? I can't help myself! I can't stop myself! I keep trying to spell potato. Is it P-O-T-A-T-O or P-O-T-A-T-O-E?

JANE

Oh, how I wish Dr. Sigmund were here! Not that he helped us very much before.

TEXT

P-O-T-A-T-O-E—that's it! I'm sure that's it.

JANE

(ignoring the Text and thinking aloud)
I can't be Jennifer again. They're on to that disguise.

TEXT

No, it's P-O-T-A-T-O.

JANE

But I'll be someone else none of those theorists would be likely to care about and so will you.
(She pauses, frowning, and then brightens.)
I know what I'll do. I'll be an old-fashioned New Critic, a formalist. I'll be Helen Vendler. And you'll be Keats's "Ode on a Grecian Urn."
(severely)
Can you manage that?

TEXT

(admiringly to Jane)
"Thou still unravished bride of quietness."

JANE

We'll take the first train out to Milan, the one I saw in my timetable yesterday.

PAN TO *a chair in the corner, where the ladies' room attendant in "her" uniform is watching Jane intently. In one hand "she" holds a tape recorder wrapped in a roll of toilet paper.*

EXT. THE WHITE HOUSE, WASHINGTON, D.C.

George and Barbara Bush are walking Millie in the Rose Garden, arguing vehemently.

GEORGE

I suppose you think it's *Millie's Book*. Well I still don't care. Sticks and stones—
                 (*He throws a stick for Millie.*)

BARBARA
       (*earnestly*)

Imagine if it's the Pledge of Allegiance, what would happen to you then?

GEORGE

(*looking first at Millie and then at the bottom of his shoe*)
Deep doo doo, dear. Deep doo doo.

BARBARA

Seriously, George—

GEORGE
       (*petulantly*)

"I know what I've told you I'm going to say, I'm going to say. And what else I say, well, I'll take some time to figure out—figure that all out."

BARBARA

I tell you what, why don't you appoint a commission to track that text down and take it under advisement?

ACT II

GEORGE

Read my lips, you Silver Fox. I'll do better than that. I'll have Lynne appoint a commission to take it into custody. "I mean, I think there'll be a lot of aftermaths in what happened, but we're going to go forward."

INT. A MICHELIN THREE-STAR IN THE FIFTH ARONDISSEMENT

Feminist theorists JANE GALLOP, HÉLÈNE CIXOUS, LUCE IRIGARAY, and JULIA KRISTEVA are lunching elegantly.

GALLOP

Scandalous. This Jane Marple presumes to "a fraudulent power" over the lost text; she refuses to acknowledge that "*écriture féminine* [may well be] lesbian cunnilingus." But those men—Derrida, Hartman, Said, Poirot—they want to appropriate our "snatches of conversation," they want us to pay "lip service" to the "phallus," even though we know that "Phallus/penis: same difference."
(*to the waiter*)
I'll have the skewered lamb à la Marquis de Sade and crushed tomatoes.

CIXOUS

"I, revolt, rages, where am I to stand? What is my place if I am a woman?"
(*to the waiter*)
I'll have a bloody steak, followed by a milkshake and "oranges."

IRIGARAY

(*sardonically*)
Little do they understand. This shadowed text is multivocal, it's a woman's text, "*always in the process of weav-*

ing itself, of embracing itself with words, but also of getting rid of words in order not to become fixed, congealed in them."

(*to the waiter*)

I'll have *liebfraumilch*. I suppose it will have to be ice cold. But I want nothing else. I can't stand solids, I only imbibe fluids.

KRISTEVA

I must differ. "*Woman as such* does not exist." You are all suffering from a biologistic, essentialist notion of femininity. That text no doubt inscribes the semiotic *chora,* refusing the thetic. It probably decenters "the transcendental ego, cutting through it, and opening it up to a dialectic in which its syntactic and categorical understanding is merely the liminary moment of the process, which is itself always acted upon by the relation to the other dominated by the death drive and its productive reiteration of the 'signifier.' "

(*to the waiter*)

I'll have cabbage soup to start, followed by suckling pig.

GALLOP

Those men. They think that "women as women, as incarnations of the Myth of Woman, do not produce culture." Let's follow them. My informant tells me (if such a univocal utterance can be trusted), that Jane Marple leaves tonight for Milan, and that Derrida along with his acolytes are all going in disguise on the same train. Whatever they can do, we can do better.

CIXOUS

(*digging into her rare steak*)

Ah the *jeu,* the *jus,* the *jouissance!* The laugh of the Medusa! We are "spacious, singing flesh!"

ACT II

GALLOP
Then what's our plan?

IRIGARAY
We know exactly what to do about this.
> (*She sips liebfraumilch.*)

"We know that women find themselves . . . proverbially, *in masquerade.*" So *we* will masquerade.

CIXOUS
She who laughs last, laughs best.

KRISTEVA
What do you mean *she?* Although—
> (*She eyes her plate.*)

"the maternal [may be] the only function of the [so-called] 'other sex' to which we can definitely attribute existence."
> (*She stabs at the suckling pig.*)

INT. THE NIGHT TRAIN TO MILAN

Jane, disguised as Helen Vendler, and the Text, disguised as Keats's "Ode on a Grecian Urn," have just been seated at one end of the dining car. Jane/Vendler is murmuring affectionately to the Text.

JANE/VENDLER
What delight I am given by your "tranquil and sovereign language," and by your "noble exploratory progress toward 'philosophizing.' "

TEXT/ODE
> (*responding with equal affection*)

"Sylvan historian, who canst thus express/A flowery tale more sweetly than our rhyme."

JANE
But what—But who—?

PAN TO *the other end of dining car. Some extremely odd-looking travelers are being shown to their tables.* ZOOM IN *on Derrida dressed as Marilyn Monroe or Madonna in spike heels and a gown made of an indeterminate number of chiffon veils and, beside "her," Hartman disguised as "her" male secretary. At a table across the aisle from them are Kristeva, impersonating a nursing mother with her infant, and Cixous, attired as a person of multiple, fluid gender identities. They are joined by Gallop, disguised as Jacques Lacan, and Irigaray, costumed as Plato. The two are quarreling over a picnic basket in which they carry the Transcendental Signifier.*

PAN BACK TO *Jane as Vendler and the Text as Ode.*

TEXT/ODE
"What men or gods are these? What maidens loth?/ What mad pursuit? What struggle to escape?"

JANE/VENDLER
Whoever they are, they seem to me to be vulgar, repellent, impertinent, and unrefined.
(*She stares hard at the other end of the dining car.*)
They are definitely *not* from Harvard.

PAN TO *Derrida, who is dictating to Hartman.*

DERRIDA
(*in an insinuating undertone*)
Me, I am woman, and I am disruptive. These days, you know, "Man and woman change places. They exchange masks *ad infinitum.*"

ACT II

HARTMAN
(*responding as he takes notes in shorthand*)
"This *Aufhebung* of the theme of castration involves a polemic with Lacan on the central role of the phallus as signifier or 'transcendental key' in the process of sexual differentiation."

PAN BACK TO *Jane and Text.*

TEXT/ODE
"Bold lover, never, never canst thou kiss,/Though winning near the goal . . ."

CUT TO *the Autostrada outside Milan. Two black stretch limos are seen speeding toward the French border.* ZOOM IN *to show William Bennett, former Drug Czar and NEH Chair, Lynne Cheney, current head of NEH, and Allan Bloom, author of* The Closing of the American Mind, *wearing dark glasses and sipping root beer in the backseat of the lead limo.*

BENNETT
Overtake that train, driver. We must repossess our lost legacy.

CUT BACK TO LONG SHOT *of the train, crossing the Alps into Italy.* ZOOM IN *on the dining car and* PAN TO *Gallop-as-Lacan and Irigaray-as-Plato, who are eavesdropping on Derrida and Hartman with alarm and interest as they tug at the picnic basket containing the Transcendental Signifier.*

GALLOP/LACAN
No one has it, you can't have it, and they can't either!

IRIGARAY/PLATO
(*sardonically*)
"The Idea of Ideas, alone, is itself in itself." Is that not so, Crito?
(*She furtively tries to open picnic basket.*)

CIXOUS/INDETERMINATE BEING
(*intervening to grab the picnic basket for herself*)
I claim this supposedly Transcendental Signifier in the name of "the *other bisexuality,* the one with which every subject, who is not shut up inside the spurious Phallocentric Performing Theater, sets up his or her erotic universe."

KRISTEVA/NURSING MOTHER
(*dreamily ignoring others as she suckles her infant while speaking in two columns*)

Column A
"FLASH—instant of time or of dream without time; inordinately swollen atoms of a bond, a vision, a shiver, a yet formless, unnameable embryo. Epiphanies. . . . Let a body venture at last out of its shelter, take a chance with meaning under a veil of words. WORD FLESH."

Column B
"Christianity is doubtless the most refined symbolic construct in which femininity, to the extent that it transpires through it—and it does so incessantly—is focused on *Maternality.*"

CUT BACK TO *Jane and the Text at the rear of the car.*

ACT II

JANE/VENDLER
(absently stroking the Text while staring nervously at the
fracas that has developed around the picnic basket)
I do hope to render you more intelligible, you and
those other "great poems, which remain 'forever warm
and still to be enjoyed.' "
(She licks her lips.)

*Suddenly there is a jolt, a screech of brakes, and all in the dining car
scream as the train lurches to an abrupt stop. ZOOM IN on entrance
to dining car, where the members of the American Presidential Commission, accompanied by Italian police, are climbing onto the train
and looking suspiciously at the disguised theorists.*

PAN TO Text and Jane still seated at the far end of the car.

TEXT/ODE
"Who are these coming to the sacrifice? . . . What little
town by river or sea shore,/Or mountain-built with
peaceful citadel,/Is emptied of this folk, this pious
morn?"

JANE/VENDLER
(hissing urgently at the Text and adjusting her Vendler
costume)
Something's happening. But no matter what, just remember, " 'Beauty is truth, truth beauty'—that is all/
Ye know on earth, and all ye need to know."

ZOOM IN on the Commission.

*The Commission, led by Lynne Cheney, William Bennett, and Allan
Bloom, is followed by two ASSISTANT PROFESSORS of Cultural
Studies. The group also includes a token black woman, Professor*

BARBARA CHRISTIAN of the University of California, Berkeley, along with a number of MLA dignitaries and former dignitaries— Jonathan Culler, CATHARINE STIMPSON, and none other than Helen Vendler herself.

BENNETT
(flashing his former Drug Czar badge)
Okay, everybody, freeze. We represent the United States government, and these *carabinieri*
(pointing to uniformed Italians)
are here to help us.
(He turns to Cheney and Bloom.)
Look at this bunch of crazies. If this isn't a gang of intellectual relativists and left-wing metaphysicians, I'm not an ex-Drug Czar and an ex-ex-smoker.

STIMPSON
(stepping forward to restrain him)
Now Bill, you know that "a virtue of American higher education has been its devotion to cultural freedom."

BLOOM
(pointing a trembling finger at Irigaray's Plato costume)
Is this the *Symposium* that I see before me?

CUT TO Jane. She is frantically and unsuccessfully trying to open the door at her end of the dining car.

JANE/VENDLER
(to Text)
What shall I do? My subject position has been usurped!

TEXT/ODE
(reassuringly)
"Beauty is truth, truth beauty."

ACT II

CUT BACK TO *the Commission. The members are feverishly arguing and gesticulating until Culler steps forward and casts a keen and practiced eye around the dining car.*

CULLER
(affably)
Ah, I see a number of my friends are here.
> *(He moves toward the veiled "woman" and "her" secretary.)*
Hi there, Jacques; good to see you, Geoffrey.
> *(Turns toward Gallop-as-Lacan, Irigaray-as-Plato, et al.)*
Hello ladies. Greetings, Jane, Luce, Hélène, and Julia.
> *(He beams at Gallop and Kristeva.)*
How are the bambini?

STIMPSON
(majestically, to all)
It is an honor and a pleasure to welcome you to this ad hoc meeting of our Commission and to solicit your assistance in our quest for a missing text.

VENDLER
The truth is, we have unfortunately lost a noble and delicious poem.
> *(She licks her lips.)*

HARTMAN
(suddenly leaping up in excitement and pointing toward the end of the car where Jane and the Text are now huddled in a corner)
My God, down there, there's been a text down there all along. Save that text!

TRACKING SHOT *as all rush toward the two.*

106

TEXT/ODE
(*shouting frantically*)
"Beauty is truth, truth beauty."

DERRIDA
(*scornfully*)
An impossibly nostalgic, undecidable, and indecipherable proposition.

CIXOUS
Phallologocentric drivel!

HARTMAN
(*triumphantly*)
Keats! Keats's "Ode on a Grecian Urn."

VENDLER
(*to the Text*)
Don't worry. I'll save you. A thing of beauty is a joy forever.

BENNETT
(*ignoring the Text and looking back and forth between the two Helen Vendlers*)
One of you is even more of a fake than most humanists nowadays.

STIMPSON
(*ceremonially*)
Will the real Helen Vendler please stand up?

DERRIDA
(*scoffing*)
Real? Reality? Are you implying a metaphysics of presence?

ACT II

IRIGARAY
(*gazing in awe at the two Helen Vendlers*)
This just proves my point. She is infinitely other in herself.

BENNETT
(*irascibly*)
Enough of this theoretical dithering.

CHENEY
(*shouldering him aside and addressing the two Vendlers as well as the Text*)
I hereby take custody of the three of you in the name of the National Endowment for the Humanities. We'll proceed from here directly to the Rockefeller Foundation's Conference Center at the Villa Serbelloni in Bellagio.

ASSISTANT PROFESSOR OF CULTURAL STUDIES
As a feminist, I object. *Sir* Belloni? What about *Madame* Belloni?

BENNETT
No matter how you slice it, it's baloney.

CAMERA PULLS BACK *to show the theorists looking disconsolate while the* carabinieri *surround the Text and the two Helen Vendlers and the American Commission files off the train and into two waiting stretch limos. The driver of the first limo eerily resembles the mysterious ladies' room attendant from the Deux Magots. "He" is speaking rapidly into a cellular phone.*

EXT. THE SPACIOUS TERRACE OF THE VILLA SERBELLONI

A butler who looks suspiciously like DAVID LODGE is serving aperitifs to the Presidential Commission and Jane. Standing off to one side, Professors Sandra Gilbert and Susan Gubar are looking at the magnificent views of Lecco and Como. PAN TO an umbrella table at the center of the terrace, where members of the Commission are taking turns interrogating the Text and the two Helen Vendlers.

BENNETT
(pointing to Helen Vendler)
I didn't trust that woman from the start. You can't trust anyone from a liberal stronghold like Harvard.

VENDLER
My dear Mr. Bennett, the only reason I'm ignoring your egregious impudence is because I consider it so crucial that we rescue this beautiful ode by Keats. Otherwise, you can be sure I'd proffer my resignation from this commission.

CHRISTIAN
(quietly)
What makes you so certain that this text is Keats's "Ode on a Grecian Urn"?

VENDLER
Obviously we would not be here if the text were some trivial work, and, speaking from its own eternity, it has told us that "beauty is truth, truth beauty." How could we doubt words of such sweetness and light?

CULLER
But of course, Helen, you'd never be so naive as to suppose that we're dealing with an utterance that is merely univocal.

STIMPSON
This text might be multiply referential and polysemous.

ACT II

ASSISTANT PROFESSOR 1
It might bear traces of the grotesque appropriation of the friezes from the Parthenon by Lord Elgin and the imperative of British Romanticism to naturalize what was in reality an act of cultural aggression.

ASSISTANT PROFESSOR 2
No, no. "Cold pastoral!" It might inscribe a relationship between fictions of tuberculosis and the opening and closing of windows that will illuminate medical discourse in nineteenth-century England.

JANE/VENDLER
(*desperately, to the Text*)
"What leaf-fring'd legend haunts about thy shape?"

TEXT/ODE
(*feebly*)
"A heart high-sorrowful and cloy'd,/A burning forehead, and a parching tongue."

CUT TO *Gilbert and Gubar leaning on a parapet and musing over their drinks.*

SG1
(*wearily*)
I say, stop the in jokes!

SG2
Yes, and besides, isn't this fetishization of academic methodologies and celebrities in any case just a reaction-formation against the marginalization of intellectuals in American life? What *is* the function of criticism at the present time?

SG1
Who do you think you are, Matilda Arnold?

SG2
(*spitefully*)
I'm shocked, shocked. Your analogies are all drawn from the usual suspects, i.e., DWMs—Dead White Men!

As the collaborators begin poking each other fretfully, ZOOM IN on a white-coated waiter with a tray of drinks. He/she is photographing the scene with a camera concealed inside a Campari soda bottle. He/she bears a bizarre resemblance to the driver of the lead limo, who in turn resembled the ladies' room attendant from the Deux Magots.

CUT BACK TO the umbrella table, where the discourse has become even more animated.

BLOOM
I continue to maintain that this is Plato's *Symposium*. The beautiful, the true, and the good. All we know and all we need to know!

ASSISTANT PROFESSOR 1
(*shouting*)
Not at all. The dialogic, the carnivalesque, the Bakhtinesque!

ASSISTANT PROFESSOR 2
(*shouting louder*)
O Foucault, wouldst thou were with us at this hour. We need your archaeology of knowledge.

ASSISTANT PROFESSOR 1
Mon Dieu, Bourdieu!

ACT II

ASSISTANT PROFESSOR 2
Bachelard! Lyotard! Baudrillard! Au Cunard!

CULLER
(*mildly, to Vendler*)
Surely it is clear that there is no reason to trust the self-asseverating claims of this linguistic field. Obviously, Helen, whether it is a text or a textlike situation, it need not necessarily be Keats's "Ode on a Grecian Urn."

VENDLER
(*with disgust*)
If you are suggesting that this text may be aesthetically naive or excessively didactic, I see no reason to save it at all. If it is not a work produced by a solitary genius, it ceases to concern me. I will withdraw at once from this commission and I trust that you, too,
(*She stares fixedly at Bennett and Cheney.*)
will encourage this lamentable and troublesome document to jump at once into the beautiful lake on which we are right now gazing.

JANE
(*involuntarily*)
O no, no, Professor Vendler. Please don't say that. I'm still hoping that we can read this Text!

All gasp and turn toward Jane with sudden understanding.

STIMPSON
(*kindly*)
Plainly, you are *not* Helen Vendler.

JANE
(*sobbing*)

It's true, it's true. I'm Jane Marple. Please help me save the Text.

BENNETT
(*to Vendler*)

My apologies, dear lady. It is a pleasure to concede that there is at least one real humanist left at Harvard.

VENDLER
(*stalking off in a rage*)

Believe me, I speak for my entire department, indeed for my institution.

CHENEY
(*taking command and sternly addressing the cowering Text*)

Now let's hope you'll listen to reason. If you're not the Pledge of Allegiance, the *Symposium,* or the "Ode on a Grecian Urn," who are you?
(*threateningly*)

You must understand that if you don't answer this question at once, there are certain measures we can take. Unpleasant ones.

JANE
(*gasping*)

What will you do?

TEXT
(*babbling in despair*)

" . . . this generation waste . . . in midst of other woe . . ."

ACT II

BENNETT
(in a sinister tone, to the Text)

Do you know what happens to texts that pretend to be more important than they really are?

(triumphantly)

They are exiled from the library and go to *Book Depositories*. There they are shelved by size, in two ranks on each shelf, and catalogued not by title, not by subject, not by author, but *only* by accession number!

(chuckles hideously)

No one will ever find you in such a place. The temperature is kept low and the lights are dimmed. In short, you will be in cold storage and in darkness perpetual!

(turns suavely to group at large)

As my colleagues are no doubt aware, there just *isn't* enough room in our libraries for all the books that have been published. Information glut.

CHRISTIAN
(stepping forward defiantly and addressing Bennett, Cheney, and Bloom)

Why are you making such a fuss about what you call "importance"? Surely by now those of us in African-American studies and Women's studies have "questioned the idea of great works of literature, preferences clearly determined by a powerful elite" and have established that "forms . . . not considered literature—for example, the diary, the journal, the letter"—need to be prized and preserved.

ASSISTANT PROFESSOR 1
(in a warmly congratulatory tone)

A marvelous multicultural point which I'm sure will facilitate your construction of a black feminist literary theory.

CHRISTIAN

Let me be frank with you. "I, for one, am tired of being asked to produce a black feminist literary theory." In my opinion, "the new emphasis on literary critical theory is as hegemonic as the world it attacks."

Jane turns hopefully toward Christian, but there is a general murmur of discontent among members of the Commission.

CULLER
(ritualistically)

Let me quote. "The resistance to theory is in fact a resistance to reading."

CHRISTIAN

"The race for theory—with its linguistic jargon; its emphasis on quoting its prophets; its tendency towards 'biblical' exegesis; its refusal even to mention specific works of creative writers, far less contemporary ones; its preoccupations with mechanical analyses of language, graphs, algebraic equations; its gross generalizations about culture—has silenced many of us to the extent that some of us feel we can no longer discuss our own literature, and others have developed intense writing blocks and are puzzled by the incomprehensibility of the language set adrift in literary circles."

JANE

Thank you, Professor Christian. That's just what I too want. Not to have a fixed method but to learn to read my Text.

BLOOM

I know your type. You're the sort of person who would assign *The Color Purple* to your classes instead of *The Symposium*.

ACT II

CUT TO *the door to the terrace. THREE MASKED TERRORISTS are efficiently gagging the David Lodge butler and pointing machine guns toward the Commission, Jane, and the Text.*

TERRORIST 1

Everybody down. Flat on your faces.

TERRORIST 2

Your text or your lives.

TERRORIST 3

We know as well as you do that this sacrilegious text is *The Satanic Verses* by Salman Rushdie.

TERRORIST 1

We are the bearers of a *fatwa* from the Ayatollah Ruhollah Khomeini: "In the name of God Almighty . . . the book entitled *The Satanic Verses* . . . has been sentenced to death."

CUT TO *Gilbert and Gubar, watching in alarm.*

SG1

Xenophobia! Blame the third world, as usual.

SG2

How do you know they're *really* the Ayatollah's emissaries? Maybe they're simply impersonating Islamic fundamentalists!

SG1

Setting up a sequel?

INT. ALISTAIR COOKE'S LIVING ROOM SET

Foreign Intrigues

The hosts of Masterpiece Theatre *are seated in their usual chairs.*

HOST 1
We hope you've enjoyed "Foreign Intrigues," this week's installment of "Masterpiece Theatre: An Academic Melodrama." We've tried tonight to introduce you to the international scene and give you some sense of the glamor that surrounds so many of the fascinating, jet-setting celebrities who make the humanities special fun for all of us.

HOST 2
Please join us next week for the exciting climax of our meta-miniseries. You'll learn the answers to the key questions that we know are haunting you right now. *Has* the Text really been captured by the Ayatollah's emissaries or were the masked terrorists employed by some of the other characters we've just met—and if so, who? And speaking of characters, who was that ladies' room attendant cum chauffeur cum waiter and was she/he trying to save or assassinate the Text? Most important of all, what will be the fate of the Text?

HOST 1
Here are some highlights from next week's concluding episode.

CUT TO A MALL IN NORTH CAROLINA

Jesse Helms is campaigning for reelection, standing on a platform festooned with life-size pictures of himself and draped in red, white, and blue.

HELMS
And I promise you folks here today, you good God-fearing Americans, that that text will be put on trial

ACT II

right here in the United States. Yes, and if it doesn't take a proper loyalty oath—and I'll betcha anything it won't!—that text will be tried, sentenced, and executed right here on American soil. We won't just ban that book, we'll burn that book, as soon as we can get it into a federal courtroom.

(*As a band in the background bursts into "Amazing Grace," he turns beaming to an aide and speaks in an undertone.*)

Best goddamn little campaign issue I've come up with for quite a while!

CUT TO THE LOBBY OF THE HOTEL URANIA, NEW YORK

A World Organization of Writers (WOW) conference is underway, with crowds of writers jostling each other on the registration line.

ZOOM IN *on Jane in a phone booth.*

JANE
(*frantically*)

Hello, hello, is this the Computer Crisis Hotline? I need help right away. I'm trying to read a text that just got trapped on a floppy disk but I don't know what program to use to open the file. What if I use Wordstar and it's in Wordperfect? Or even in Nota Bene? My God, I might erase it entirely! Or it could come down with a virus!

CUT BACK TO MASTERPIECE THEATRE'S LIVING ROOM SET

The hosts of the show are seated, with the usual baroque music swelling in the background.

HOST 1

Tonight's episode of *Masterpiece Theatre* has been brought to you through a grant from De-signer Signs,

*Un*limited, a worldwide chain of boutiques disseminating postmodern masks and masquerades for the theoretical sophisticate, with the motto "Style or Stylus, Same Difference" and the theme song "Amazing Gaze."

HOST 2

We are also grateful for assistance from Ortho-Think, Inc., the makers of PC for your PC, a software program that lets you check your text for its political correctness, with the motto "I'm right; you're almost certainly hegemonic." In support of tonight's program, Ortho-Think is pleased to offer a special challenge to viewers: "Buy a margin, get a center." Good night.

ACT III

The *Final Deletion*; or, *Bookworms* in the *Big Apple*

INT. ALISTAIR COOKE'S LIVING ROOM SET

Hosts are seated in front of a large tank containing strange-looking fish.

HOST 1

Good evening. And welcome back to *Masterpiece Theatre*. Yet again, we're honored to be sitting in for the indefatigable Alistair Cooke, who has this week journeyed to Cape Canaveral to cover the historic launching of our nation's first permanent space station, the *Priapus I*. Tonight we'll be bringing you the thrilling climax of this season's run of our pioneering documetadrama, "Masterpiece Theatre: An Academic Melodrama."

HOST 2

As you'll remember, in our last episode, Jane and her companion, the baffled Text, were fleeing across Europe from a sinister assortment of Marxists, postcolonialists, feminist theorists, deconstructionists, and, yes, traditionalists when they were captured by a blue-ribbon presidential Commission and brought to the Rockefeller Foundation's Study and Conference Center at the Villa Serbelloni in Bellagio. There, to the horror of all, the Text was seized by three masked terrorists, who claimed that it was *The Satanic Verses* by Salman Rushdie and that they were emissaries from the Ayatollah Khomeini.

HOST 1

How can the hapless Text possibly escape such ruthless assassins? And, even if it does, what new perils might await young Jane and her besieged comrade?

HOST 2

As this final episode begins, Jane has just arrived in the Big Apple, where she is registering for a WOW—World Organization of Writers—Conference at the Hotel Urania.

SOUND OVER: *horns honking, sirens blaring, jackhammers drilling, smash of wrecking balls, and screams from the street.*

HOST 1

Surely, among those who live by the word, our hero will find allies in her battle to save the Text from extermination.

HOST 2

Or will she?

SOUND OVER: *squealing brakes followed by gunshots.*

INT. THE POSH LOBBY OF THE HOTEL URANIA, CURRENTLY BEING RENOVATED

Half is decorated in late Victorian crimsons and golds, with over-stuffed sofas, potted plants, Oriental rugs, and crystal chandeliers. Behind a maze of plywood dividers, the other half is emerging as a

ACT III

high-tech postmodern space of halogen lighting, chrome and leather chairs, polished slate tiles, and abstract neon artworks. Long lines of bedraggled, tormented-looking writers—some attired in native costumes, others in jeans, and still others in vivid designer ensembles— spiral through the plywood maze leading to the registration desk.

ZOOM IN *on an exhausted Jane, approaching the registration desk accompanied by none other than David Lodge.*

JANE
It's so good of you to have helped me change places.

LODGE
(*gallantly*)
Well, it was nice work being a butler at the Villa Serbelloni—I like to be able to "observe things in anonymity" and I get "a charge out of the double life"— but it was nicer work still to get you out of there.

JANE
It's lucky for me that when I was dragged to the Villa by the Commissioners, you were already there researching the foibles of scholars-in-residence for your next novel.

LODGE
(*modestly*)
"For me academia is what bullfighting was for Hemingway."

JANE
Well you certainly fooled those maddened bulls Bennett and Bloom when you told them to go hunt for the Text and the terrorists in the grottos of the Villa garden! They really believed you were the butler so they just assumed you knew where to look.

LODGE

I must admit, though, that my best plot device was the one about the dentist. Or should I say dentists? Along with death, dentists may be "the only idea you can't deconstruct. Work back from there and you end up with the old idea of the autonomous self."

JANE

I certainly felt a lot more autonomous when we got to that so-called dentist in Como, even though I was still scared about the Text and the gunmen.

LODGE

You see, I thought it inadvisable to explain things to you until . . .

FLASHBACK TO ONE OF THE SIDE CHAPELS IN THE COMO DUOMO

A bank of votive candles placed before a small altar to the Virgin flickers in the gloom. Eerie organ music rises from the front of the cathedral.

Three shadowy figures detach themselves from a camera-bearing, shopping bag-laden mass of Japanese tourists admiring a nearby tapestry and slip into the chapel where Jane and David Lodge stand together.

JANE
(*wonderingly*)
And so you really *are* David Lodge! But why have you brought me here?

LODGE
Let the "terrorists" tell you for themselves.

ACT III

JANE
Oh my God. You mean *you*—

Jane looks around in alarm, searching for terrorists, as the first of the three shadowy figures comes forward into the circle of candle-light.

TERRORIST 1
(unwrapping a long silk scarf from around "his" head)
I am Isabel Allende. I wanted to help save your text because in the part of the world I come from many of us treasure words, so much so that throughout South America you can ride on a bus for free or get a cup of coffee gratis if you are able to recite a poem.

TERRORIST 2
(unwrapping a similar scarf)
I am Buchi Emecheta. I joined with the others to smuggle your text out of the Villa on a terrifyingly tiny sailboat because the manuscript of my first novel, *The Bride Price,* was burned by my husband and because even now there are too many ambitious Nigerian women who pay a high price for being brides.

TERRORIST 3
(also unwrapping a scarf)
I am Bharati Mukherjee and I have Federal Expressed your text to you at the Hotel Urania in New York, where a WOW conference begins the day after tomorrow, because, like Isabel and Buchi, I have experienced writing as "a compulsive act ... a kind of salvation. ... People like me, because we've come from the Third World [know that a] social and political vision is an integral part of writing a novel, of being a novelist."

JANE
(*dumbfounded*)
Would Aunt Jane have predicted that the three helper figures would be three third-world women?
(*She turns to Lodge.*)
Or do you think I'm suffering from delusions of political correctness?

ALLENDE
This is no hallucination. Sometimes "I feel like words are choking me, that I will die if I don't write. . . . I think that the world is a crazy place, very unjust and unfair and violent, and I'm angry at that. I want to change the rules, change the world."

EMECHETA
And I—after I learned "to use tools for the same art" of storytelling that my mother had mastered—was told by my teacher "Miss Humble" to "pray for God's forgiveness." But "my Chi's voice suddenly grew louder, so loud that it covered that of Miss Humble" and I realized that "God had more important things to do than to start punishing me for speaking my dreams aloud."

LODGE
(*diffidently to Jane*)
This is not as romantic as you think. It just happens that I have here a booklet of super saver coupons that will get us on a plane out of Milan to the WOW meeting in New York tomorrow morning.

JANE
But how can we keep those creepy Commissioners at the Villa off our tracks?

ACT III

LODGE

Root canal. I'll tell them the Como dentist isn't up to it—or do I mean down to it?—so I'm taking you to Milan because you've had a terrible abscess.

MUKERJEE

Just ask for a Fed Ex in your name at the registration desk of the Hotel Urania. Your text will be waiting for you there.

CUT BACK TO *the Hotel Urania. Jane approaches the registration desk, where writers are shouting at the hotel clerk.*

WRITER 1

Are you sure I don't have a fax from Hollywood? Could you look again?

PUBLISHER 1

Where's the Exhibit Hall? I've got to start setting up my display of our new Serial Killer Trading Cards.

WRITER 2
(*to Writer 3*)

They promised me that the sweatshirt contract for my sequel to *The Last Temptation of Christ* would be here by now.

REPORTER 1

Can you tell me where Allen Ginsberg is going to do his Nostalgia Now! reading of *Howl?* I'm profiling him for *Rolling Stone.*

WRITER 4

I insist on protesting the display of *Heather Has Two Mommies* at this event. Everybody knows it gives vulnerable kids the wrong ideas about family values.

The Final Deletion

REPORTER 2

Can you tell me Shirley MacLaine's room number? I'm here to interview her for the *Madame Sosostris Society Newsletter.*

JANE

(interrupting, to the clerk, as she pushes her registration card forward) .
Do you have a Federal Express package for me?
(She looks meaningfully at David Lodge.)

DESK CLERK

Just a minute. I'll check.

PHOTOGRAPHER 1

Hey, I need to get some shots of the Rock Bottom Remainders—the band of authors that's going to play tonight after the Ginsberg reading. Maybe you could just give me the room numbers of Amy Tan, their singer, and Stephen King, their guitarist.

DESK CLERK

(shoving two Fed Ex envelopes toward Jane)
You have two, actually. Could you please sign both slips?

ZOOM IN *on Jane as she fumbles in her purse for a pen.* PULL BACK *to long shot of writers, reporters, and photographers shouting and scrabbling around her.* ZOOM IN *on counter as a mysterious hand reaches out, deftly removes one of the Fed Ex envelopes, and replaces it with another.*

JANE

(flushed and excited, to the desk clerk)
Oh, thank you so much for holding these. I'm really glad you guys are so efficient.

LODGE
(*smugly*)
I told you so. It's truly a small world and one in which happy endings *are* possible.

<u>INT</u>. A PENTHOUSE SUITE AT THE HOTEL URANIA

The suite's TV screen fills our screen with an image of a trench-coated Dan Rather standing outside the State Department, speaking rapidly into a microphone and gazing earnestly into the camera.

RATHER
There's no consensus here at Foggy Bottom. One highly placed source told me this afternoon that the textnap probably was the work of the Ayatollah's emissaries. But several others disagreed, with a few casting suspicion on Saddam Hussein and others hinting at PLO involvement. It's possible, according to one Washington expert on Middle Eastern affairs, that the Ayatollah's enemies are trying to whip up Western sentiment against him by pinning the blame on him for this outrageous act of aggression against our country. All we know for now is that somewhere an innocent American text is being held hostage. Yellow ribbons have already begun to appear at Waldenbooks and B. Dalton. Later tonight a rally outside the Library of Congress in support of the captive text will be led by Gertrude Himmelfarb and Jacques Barzun.

CUT TO *the control panel of the TV. A female hand reaches out to switch off the set.* PULL BACK *to* LONG SHOT *of the suite living room, where William Bennett, Lynne Cheney, and retro-thinkers* CAROL IANONE, DINESH D'SOUZA, *and* CAMILLE PAGLIA *are gathered in front of the TV.*

The Final Deletion

CHENEY

That should distract her. It's lucky that Dick was able to get his operatives at the State Department to leak those stories.

BENNETT
(to Paglia)

You really are a woman warrior. You did a great job tracking that dupe Jane Marple and her p.c. text all through Europe. I was impressed when you disguised youself as a ladies' room attendant in Paris but even more impressed when you turned yourself into male characters, like the chauffeur and the waiter.

PAGLIA
(ruefully, eating clams on the half-shell)

It was tough going in that ladies' room, I can tell you. "Women, like female dogs, are earth-bound squatters"— no "arc of transcendence" there. And I got pretty sick to my stomach.
(She shudders.)
"The fatty female body is a sponge." But ever since I dressed up in my youth as Napoleon and the toreador from *Carmen*, I've enjoyed being a man. "I see the world from male eyes. . . . I have a long history of punching and kicking."

D'SOUZA

That text must be expunged. Since Camille discovered that it was Fed Exed to Miss Marple here, we can find it and blot it out now. I'm sure it's a new syllabus or curriculum—multicultural, postcolonial, deconstructionist rot—that will be inflicted as an "illiberal education" on our best and brightest student minds. "Resistance on campus to the academic revolution is

ACT III

outgunned and sorely needs outside reinforcements."
We can provide those reinforcements.
    (*He turns to Paglia, squeamishly.*)
Must you keep eating those clams?

IANONE

Yes, that text is probably an example of "The Political-Literary Complex," or maybe the rantings produced by "The Barbarism of Feminist Scholarship."

PAGLIA

    (*slurping down another clam as D'Souza winces*)
The "feminists are really deluded, with their heads up their ass—"

BENNETT

Here's the plan. Lynn and I will have our people search Marple's room while you two keep close tabs on her every move. As soon as we get our hands on that text, we'll off it, one way or another.

D'SOUZA

    (*petulantly to Paglia*)
Why must you keep eating those clams?

PAGLIA

"Dionysus' female chthonian swamp is inhabited by silent, swarming invertebrates. I propose that the taboo attached to women is justified and that the infamous 'uncleanness' of menstruation is due not to blood but to uterine jellies in that blood. The primal swamp is choked with menstrual albumen, the lukewarm matrix of nature, teeming with algae and bacteria. We have a food that symbolizes this swamp: raw clams on the half-shell." I adore raw clams.

The Final Deletion

<u>INT</u>. JANE'S SMALL, DARK ROOM ON THE THIRD FLOOR OF THE HOTEL URANIA

Jane and David Lodge are sitting side by side on the edge of the bed, eagerly contemplating the Federal Express envelopes.

JANE
(opening the first envelope)
Funny, this one seems to be from Boondock. God, it's from the dean's office.
(She frowns.)

LODGE
Anything wrong?

JANE
I can't believe it. I'm "not being retained" in the English department. I guess that means I'm being fired.

LODGE
But why?

JANE
(frowning more deeply)
This letter says they aren't required to give reasons, but Dean Petty adds a final paragraph saying . . . Well, here, let me quote it. "Unfortunately your misguided activism in behalf of a single aberrant text appears to have prevented you from making significant contributions in the three key areas of Research, Teaching, and Service as outlined on page twenty-four of *The Faculty Handbook's* 'Rules for Retention, Tenure, and Promotion.' Therefore we have no alternative but to terminate you forthwith. With all best wishes for your

future career, J. Arnold "Jack" Petty, Dean of the College."

LODGE

Bloody bad luck!
(*He turns to pat her reassuringly on the shoulder but is stopped by the look of horror on her face as she peers into the second Fed Ex envelope.*)

JANE

The Text. It's not here. Just some weird note.

ZOOM IN *on small page in Jane's hand. The note fills the screen, its print made up of words and letters in different sizes obviously cut from newspapers and magazines.*

> JANE MARPLE —
> GiVE It Up! sTop TrYIng to
> SAve THe TEXT! OR ELse
> whAt's IN THiS EnvELOPE
> is ALl THeRE WiLL bE.

JANE

My God, what—?
(*She shakes the envelope frantically and a single enigmatic Glyph falls into her lap. She begins to weep hysterically.*)
This is too much, just too much.

LODGE
(*intervening authoritatively*)
Take a look at this envelope. The airbill hasn't been stamped, which means—

JANE
That it wasn't sent from Italy?

LODGE
Right. This must have been hand delivered in New York.

JANE
(*wiping her eyes and then staring hard at the airbill*)
Look. Down here. There's a trace of a signature in the wrong spot.
(*She begins spelling it out.*)
R-M-C-G-U.

LODGE
(*slowly reading over her shoulder*)
R. McGuffin! Seems as if somebody was writing over the carbon—maybe without even knowing it.

JANE
(*leaping up excitedly*)
It's a lead. I'll track it down here in New York.
(*She pauses, looking nervous.*)
But what about Buchi, Isabel, and Bharati? Is it possible that they . . . ? What could have gone wrong?

LODGE
(*decisively*)
I'll have to go back to Como. I hate to think that one or all of those three . . . But I'd better find out!

ACT III

JANE
(*gazing down at the Glyph from her lost Text*)
Will I ever be able to read you now?
(*She places it carefully back in its envelope.*)

A tiny, cryptic humming rises from the torn Glyph.

INT. THE PENTHOUSE SUITE AT THE HOTEL URANIA

The TV screen fills our screen with an image of TED KOPPEL on Nightline, *about to start a discussion between the novelists ERICA JONG and BRETT EASTON ELLIS about the rally to free the hostage text that occurred earlier that evening.*

KOPPEL
Before introducing our guests tonight, let's fill in the newest developments in what has become known as Operation Inkwell, the government's effort to retrieve the hostage text. Hot off the wires right now—a report that sources at the Pentagon are claiming the missing text is not in Iran at all but instead has been taken to New York, where Mafia involvement is suspected.
(*Pictures of Erica Jong in diaphonous chiffon and Brett Easton Ellis in black leather fill the screen.*)
Erica? Brett? When we get back, I'm going to be asking each of you to speculate on the panic that seems to surround the disappearance of one little text. Why should anyone care anyway? But first a word from our local sponsor.

Images of glamorous, skimpily clad women appear on the screen while a female voice-over croons seductively: "Girls, girls, girls! Every shade, shape, sex, and flavor! Call us now at 1-900-SEX-CHAT to talk to the mistress of your dreams."

A male hand reaches out and switches off the set. PULL BACK *to a* LONG SHOT *of the suite's living room, in which Fredric Jameson, the punk author* KATHY ACKER, *two* "LANGUAGE POETS," *and a* POSTMODERNIST, POSTFEMINIST *CRITIC of popular culture are sitting in front of the screen.*

JAMESON
Nostalgic narrativizing, even though uncertainty, unknowability, and indeterminacy are the postmodern condition, as I've been arguing for years.

ACKER
(rolling up her sleeves to reveal elaborate tattoos)
"Fuck art," I say and fuck that text too. "Fuck shit prick—that's my way of talking."

JAMESON
(looking grim)
In effect, as Lyotard has observed, "the grand narrative has lost its credibility, regardless of what mode of unification it uses, regardless of whether it is a speculative narrative or a narrative of emancipation." In a culture of appropriation, commodification, and specious unification, we mustn't just thematize incoherence, we must enact it.

ACKER
That's why I plagiarize. As I've said, "I never write anything new." Originality is a bourgeois capitalist plot. So is narrative. "Get rid of meaning. Your mind is a nightmare that has been eating you: now eat your mind."

LANGUAGE POET 1
"In the process of writing what does not then occur in the head is a distraction. Why imitate 'speech'? Various

vehicle that American speech is in the different mouths of any of us possessed of particular powers of colloquial usage, rhythmic pressure, etc., it is *only such."*

POSTMOD, POSTFEM CRITIC
(*solemnly agreeing*)

Even AIDS is no more than a function of the representation of AIDS in the discourse of a bankrupt medical establishment that must produce the literal as a figure of the desire for a literality beyond rhetoricity.

ACKER
(*heatedly disagreeing and flexing her muscles*)

Nonsense. For me, the literal is revolutionary. "For me tattooing is very profound. . . . The tattooist is the tattooist. The tattooist is *my* tattooist. I'm very heavily tattooed."

LANGUAGE POET 1
"I HATE SPEECH."

JAMESON

We're agreed then. We must find this text and fracture it so that it will accord with the postmodern condition.

ACKER

Down with the text! Down with the critics! Down with the academy! "The most important men in the world decide it's their duty to tear the mother away from her child. They want to keep the child so they can train the child to suck their cocks. That's what's known as education."

JAMESON

We'll fragment ourselves, disperse all over the hotel, and make that text postmodern.

ACKER
(parodically)
WOW! "Hello, I'm Erica Jong. I'm a real novelist. I write books that talk to you about the agony of American life, how we all suffer, the growing pains that more and more of us are going to feel."

LANGUAGE POET 2
"Most words just echoes, corpses."

INT. THE JOB INFORMATION BULLETIN BOARD, STRATE-GICALLY POSITIONED JUST OUTSIDE THE PARADISO BALL-ROOM, WHERE THE MAIN MEETINGS OF THE WOW CONFER-ENCE WILL TAKE PLACE

ZOOM IN *on the center of the bulletin board. The writhing Text has been pinned up like a purloined letter. Job seekers mill about, reading ads aloud and taking notes, oblivious to the agony of the crucified Text.*

JOB SEEKER 1
Goddamn. Here's something. "East Jesus State, Dry Bones, Nevada, seeks established fiction writer (at least two published novels) for a one-semester, non–tenure track lectureship. Three-course load: one creative writing, one remedial comp, one Interdisciplinary Approaches to Medieval Studies. Salary negotiable, within the range of $7 to 9,000. We are an Equal Opportunity, Affirmative Action employer."

JOB SEEKER 2
Wait a minute. This one's a possibility too. "Walden Pond Prep in Des Moines, Iowa, will hire a resident poet who can also double as dorm counselor and ice

hockey coach. Ten months a year, three-year position. No fringe benefits available at this time. Please submit CV and portfolio of at least ten publications, plus ice hockey video. Salary $6,500 a year, along with room and board. Don't call us, we'll call you."

TEXT
(groaning and whimpering)
"Why then Ile fit you. Hieronimo's mad again" . . . "Fah, there's the burning pit."

JOB SEEKER 3
What about this? "Harvard University requires African-Am Blues and 'Be-Bop' artist to initiate new course in ethno-literary-musicology studies. Nontraditional backgrounds welcomed, though doctorate and evidence of publication necessary. Salary competitive, tenure unlikely. Send all materials to Helen Vendler, Chair of the Search Committee. Harvard really is an Equal Opportunity Affirmative Action Employer."

TEXT
(shouting)
"Mene, mene, tekel upharsin!" Or do I mean, "Eloi Eloi, lama sabachthani?" "Darkling I listen" . . . "Shantih Shantih Shantih?" . . . "I must be wicked to deserve such pain."

JOB SEEKER 1
(to Job Seeker 2)
At least there's some stuff here we can apply for. I've gotten sick of working in the mailroom at Exxon.

JOB SEEKER 2
And I really bombed the LSATS.

TEXT
"A fin in a waste of waters" . . . "Daddy, daddy you bastard, I'm through."

PULL BACK *to show a young couple approaching the bulletin board. They are Scott and Jennifer from Boondock State, both now attired in yuppie urban clothing. Jennifer wears an Ann Taylor suit with a silk blouse and Scott a J. Press navy blazer with khaki trousers. Jennifer is talking animatedly as they arrive at the board.*

JENNIFER
Oh Scott, what would I do without you? You're really getting to know the New York literary scene. It's excellent, it's mega-great.

SCOTT
(with feigned nonchalance)
Mega-boring. All those *People* mag celebs are just folks like us, Jen. Down-home dull. Let's see what kinds of opportunities you'll have if you do decide to go for that MFA.

JENNIFER
Honestly, Scott, my life has definitely been changed ever since Professor Marple explained to me what that weird text meant to her. Now I just want to become a writer myself.

TEXT
"They give birth astride of a grave" . . . "I must go on I can't go on I'll go on" . . . "Is it time for my medicine?"

ACT III

JENNIFER
(*musing over the board*)

Hey, Scott, this looks great. East Jesus State, Walden Pond Prep, Harvard University—Mom and Dad will be thrilled to hear about all these options. They keep on thinking I'll have to be a cocktail waitress if I stay in the program.

SCOTT

I don't know, Jen. Some of these academics are pretty weird. Get a load of this "personal" up here. A wild and crazy guy—*not*.

PERSONAL

TENURED FIFTYSOMETHING N.Y. ACADEMIC DW(J)M seeks ISFP (introverted, sensing, feeling, perceiving), non-smoking female *without children or pets* for regression, shamanism, spicy food, and green-speak. Must have teeth. No deconstructionists, please. Write, fax, Fed Ex, or otherwise inscribe your secret, subtextual desires to Box 2001, *Lingua Franker*.

JENNIFER
(*shrugging*)

So? *Some* older men are starting to get with it!

TEXT

"Ding dong, ding dong" . . . "I'll come to meet you as far as Cho Fu Sa" . . . "On the bald street breaks the blank day."

JENNIFER

But what's this funny thing over here? It looks so familiar.

TEXT

"Down their carved names the raindrop crawls" . . .
"No worse there is none."

JENNIFER

My God, why it's—

SCOTT

Can it be?

JENNIFER

It's Ms. Marple's text—I'm sure it is—and it looks like
it's in worse trouble than ever.

TEXT

"Pitched past pitch of grief" . . . "The rag and bone
shop of the heart."

JENNIFER

We've got to get help right away. Where should we go?
There must be some kind of headquarters here!

SCOTT
(*slowly*)
Hold on, Jen. We've got to think.

TEXT

"This strange disease of modern life" . . . "Beauty,
truth" . . . "Solid flesh . . . Dissolve. Into. A dew" . . .
"Adieux."

JENNIFER

I don't care what you say. I'm going to get help right
away.

ACT III

(*even more slowly*)
Hey, maybe my boss, Mr. McGuffin, can do something about it.

Okay. You can try that too. But I'm going to find out who's in charge here and talk to them now. Haven't you been watching the news? We're right in the middle of Operation Inkwell and this is my first big break as a journalist.

I've got to stay here and hand out a stack of information packets for the office all morning. But why don't we meet for lunch at that little Thai place across the street?

"The shadow knows" . . . "Pepsi Cola Hits the Spot" . . . "pinned and wriggling on the wall" . . . "fuck shit prick."

INT. THE HYPERION ROOM OF THE HOTEL URANIA

A meeting of WOW's American host committee is in session. NORMAN MAILER is at the head of the table, flanked by ALICE WALKER, ISHMAEL REED, JOYCE CAROL OATES, ADRIENNE RICH, and STEPHEN KING.

(*pounding on the table*)
Enough about this stupid Operation Inkwell. *Our* books are all safe. Where's Erica? She's always late.

WALKER
(*between her teeth*)
Stop trying to distract us from the main point, Norman. *You've* stuck us with this so-called "debate" this afternoon.

OATES
(*mildly*)
It *is* scandalous, Norman. A public confrontation between Kitty Kelly and Nancy Reagan! How can you call that literary? It's just gossippy sensationalism.
(*aside*)
Although it might be the germ of a good new novel, I must admit.

RICH
As a lesbian-feminist-activist-poet-essayist who would never presume to speak for but remains sensitive to the concerns and issues of women of color in a compulsively heterosexual, white, male-dominated state, I must remind you that these two white upper-class purportedly heterosexual women are not women of color.

MAILER
(*to himself*)
I'm not going to be "pussywhipped" about the ladies Kelly and Reagan.
(*to the group*)
After all, Allen Ginsberg is the star attraction at tonight's general session.
(*to himself again*)
"Matters like homosexuality and onanism are obsessive."

ACT III

REED
(*staring hard at Walker*)
Mumbo jumbo. "Writin' is fightin'." Mumbo-jumbo will hoo-doo *you*.

WALKER
(*staring at the ceiling*)
Your reckless eyeballing can't scare me, Ishmael. I'm suddenly flashing on my "spiritual colors"—turquoise and coral. I am "indescribably happy" about "the persistence of these colors in my psyche." I am "walking in a circle of magic." This strengthens me to protest Norman's plan to slander womanists everywhere.

OATES
It's shocking, really. Not just Kitty Kelly versus Nancy Reagan but Jackie Onassis on editing that new biography of Marilyn Monroe!
(*aside*)
Which might, of course, also provide some interesting material for another book.

MAILER
"It is my understanding of Marilyn Monroe that she was murderous." But what can you expect of someone who, having a "voluptuous figure and no neck, was not free of the desire to be elegant?"

KING
(*shuddering*)
Murderous. You're right. "People in general scare me. That's why I live in isolation in a remote area of Maine. I'm afraid of choking to death. I'm afraid of the San Andreas fault. I don't sleep on my left side because that's where my heart is. I'm afraid it will wear out too

quickly. I also have a recurring dream about the lake next to my house boiling and blowing up."

RICH

As a lesbian-feminist-activist-Jewish daughter of anti-Semitic southerners who gave me a training in "verbal privilege" about which I feel considerable ambivalence, I'm not scared of Marilyn Monroe or of people in general, but I *am* scared of 2-Live-Crew, and I protest your insistence on building a session around them, Norman.

REED
(staring hard at Rich)
Mumbo jumbo. "Writin' is fightin'." Mumbo-jumbo will hoo-doo *you.*

RICH
(combatively)
"In the mystique of the overpowering, all-conquering male sex drive, the penis-with-a-life-of-its own, is rooted the law of male sex right to women."

MAILER
(plaintively)
A "firm erection on a delicate fellow is man's finest moral product." Even Erica was sold on the idea of the "zipless fuck." And where in the hell is she anyway?

KING
(unexpectedly interjecting)
Another thing. I'm scared of my guitar. I'm scared of playing in the Rock Bottom Remainders. I'm even scared of this theme we seem to have.
(shivering)

ACT III

What is it, again? The word and the world? The word *of* the world? The word *in* the world? The word *as* the world? The word *against* the world?

MAILER
(*ecstatically*)

"Writers may be the last humans to enflame themselves with words. . . . Let us return to the war and the play of words that will yet show our battered wife of a world some glimpse of starlight in the aesthetic heavens."

RICH
(*shocked*)

Battered wife?

Suddenly there is a pounding at the door, and Jennifer enters, feverishly excited.

JENNIFER

Excuse me. I hate to interrupt, but you're the host committee, aren't you? You won't believe what I just found. Operation Inkwell! I found the text they're all looking for!

MAILER
(*patronizingly*)

Who are *you*? How do you know you found the right text?

RICH
(*interrupting*)

As a North American woman who was once the age of this young person, I protest your treatment of her, and as a revisionary student of "lies, secrets, and silences," I protest your use of the word "right."

JENNIFER
(*frantically*)
The job information center! The bulletin board! It's right there, out in the open, just the way it was when I first saw it in Boondock.

WALKER
Praise the spirits! My turquoise and coral were magic omens.
(*to Oates, confidentially*)
Also I have been receiving signs from the animals.

OATES
(*to herself*)
This *would* make a good novel.

KING
"Terrible things happen in the world, but they're things no one can explain."

JENNIFER
Please come with me. Come right away. I'll show you just where it is!

MAILER
Ah, the war and the play of words! Let's go.

As all rise, still quarreling among themselves, the door opens again and Erica Jong makes a belated entrance.

JONG
"Hello, I'm Erica Jong. I'm a real novelist. I write books that talk to you about the agony of American life . . ."

INT. THE LUXURIOUS THIRTIETH-FLOOR OFFICES OF MCGUFFIN BROTHERS, ON MADISON AVENUE

ACT III

ESTABLISHING SHOT *of a discreet sign on the door: "R. McGuffin Bros., Media Management and Publicity." ZOOM IN on Jane sitting in the waiting room, clutching the Fed Ex airbill.*

JANE
(*to herself*)

I'll cry tomorrow. But in the meantime this seems to be the only R. McGuffin in New York who would have anything at all to do with texts.

> (*She sighs, rises, and goes over to the RECEPTIONIST, a Marilyn Monroe look-alike in turquoise and coral.*)

Excuse me, but I've been waiting for almost an hour now. Could you please tell Mr. McGuffin I'm here about something very urgent?

RECEPTIONIST

I told you you'd be lucky if they'd see you at all. These men are two of the busiest men in New York. Hey, look, they handle Hollywood, they handle MTV, they do the glossies and the pulps, they do all the spin-offs and all the deals. Why right now they have Danielle Steel on one location, Madonna on another, and Shirley MacLaine over at the Hotel Urania.

JANE
(*lowering her voice*)

Maybe you could tell them I'm here about Operation Inkwell. It's really important.

RECEPTIONIST
(*brightening*)

You mean what was on *Nightline* last night? Okay, I'll see what I can do.

LONG SHOT *of Jane returning to her seat as the door opens and DANIELLE STEEL sweeps in, accompanied by two PUBLICITY FLACKS.*

148

The Final Deletion

STEEL
(*gushily, to the receptionist*)
Penny darling, it was so romantic. They had me posing outside the Tunnel of Love with the wind in my hair. We'll sell a million copies of *Tunnel of Love,* and I think the perfume contract will work out too. How do you like the name *Steel Magnolia?*

FLACK 1
You dropped your fan, Miss Steel.

FLACK 2
What's this?
(*He picks up a piece of paper and reads aloud.*)
"To the only man who has ever brought thunder and lightning and rainbows into my life. It happens once, and when it does, it's forever. To my one and only love, with all my heart, beloved Popeye. I love you. Olive."

STEEL
(*patting her eyes with a lace handkerchief*)
That's the dedication for my next novel, *Passion in Purple.*

RECEPTIONIST
Oh Miss Steel, I'm so glad it went well. Let me take you in right away. Rob and Rich will both want to see you.

Long shot of receptionist leading Steel and company toward inner offices. Messengers come and go, bringing in takeout foods, packages, and Fed Ex envelopes. When the room is empty, Jane slips over to the receptionist's desk and studies a large office appointment calendar. ZOOM IN on calendar. TIGHT SHOT of final item: 7 P.M., Ginsberg reading, Paradiso Ballroom, Hotel Urania.

149

ACT III

LONG SHOT *of waiting room. Door opens. Enter a gum-chewing MADONNA dressed in a tuxedo, followed by seven male dancers in trench coats over bullet bras and fishnet stockings.*

MADONNA
(*shouting*)
Penny? Hey, where's Penny? You a new girl?
(*She doesn't pause for an answer.*)
Well tell your fuck shit prick bosses Rob and Rich that I have to see them *subito*. I'm going to pussywhip both of them, but *bad*.

JANE
(*flustered*)
I'm sorry, but I'm not—

MADONNA
You tell those sons of bitches I can justify my love in any way I want. If I want to fuck a swan on camera, I'll goddamn well fuck a swan on camera. Besides, it's a classical theme. Leda and the swan.
(*She cracks her gum.*)
Who do those assholes think they are, censoring the classics?

In the background the seven dancers begin thrusting pelvises, boogying and vogueing sardonically.

MADONNA
(*censoriously*)
That's enough, boys.
(*She turns back to Jane.*)
Don't get them wrong. They're just playful. The whole troupe agrees on this, and we'll fight any censorship of our stuff, especially our video stuff. Rob and Rich are

just like all straight men. They "need to be emascu-
lated. I'm sorry. They all need to be slapped around."

*As Madonna is speaking, a group of people emerge from the inner
offices and split up as soon as they take in the scene. One elegantly
attired man, clearly a MCGUFFIN BROTHER, obsequiously escorts
Danielle Steel and her flacks out to the lobby, while another, clearly
also a MCGUFFIN BROTHER, immediately goes over to Madonna
and tries to hug her.*

MADONNA
(*pulling away*)

"Every straight guy should have a man's tongue in his
mouth at least once." My boys and I are here to see that
you get that pleasure today, aren't we boys?

MCGUFFIN
(*attempting but not bringing off a chuckle*)

Wonderful to see you, sweetie.

MADONNA

Cut the crap, big Mac. My new video. You let those
bastards mangle it.

MCGUFFIN

You've heard about the cuts but you haven't heard
about the deal!

MADONNA

I don't give a—

JANE
(*interrupting*)

Excuse me, Mr. McGuffin, but I told your receptionist
to tell you I'm here about—

ACT III

MCGUFFIN
(*impatiently*)

I know nothing about it. Nothing whatever. Sorry, I have nothing to say.

JANE
(*thrusting the airbill toward him*)

But what about this? Your name.

MCGUFFIN

Lots of people know my name. My name is big business.

MADONNA
(*after sticking her finger in her mouth as if to vomit*)

Hey, let's get back to the point. When is a swan not a swan? When its feathered glory is between *my* loosening thighs!

JANE
(*earnestly, ignoring Madonna*)

But Mr. McGuffin, a text is missing. You must have heard about it on *Nightline,* and here's your name on this airbill that came to me with an empty envelope where my text was supposed to be.

MCGUFFIN
(*to Madonna*)

Darling, baby, I can explain.
(*to Jane*)

Try the studios. Everybody at the studios knows my name. One of those creeps must have forged it.

JANE

Studios? Which studios?

MCGUFFIN

That bastard David Lynch, for starters. He's had it in for me ever since I told him the second season of *Twin Peaks* wouldn't fly.

(*to Madonna, and gesturing toward dancers*)

Come on. Let's get all these beautiful twin peaks into my office.

INT. THE JOB INFORMATION BULLETIN BOARD

The Text is continuing its mad monologue.

TEXT

"I felt a funeral in my brain" ... "Good night ladies, good night sweet ladies" ... "Bababaadalgharaghta-kamminarronnkonnbronntonnerronntuonnthrunntr ovarrhounawnskawntoohoohooordenenthurnuk!"

TIGHT SHOT *of Text as a mysterious hand reaches out and removes it from the board, replacing it with a shiny REPLICANT.*

LONG SHOT *of Jennifer and the WOW host committee rushing toward the bulletin board and then massed in front of it.*

JENNIFER

(*clearly dismayed*)

My God, that's not it at all. Not what I saw at all.

MAILER

(*sternly*)

Is this your idea of a joke, young lady? *Cliff Notes* on *Hamlet?* Surely our government hasn't mounted Operation Inkwell to retrieve those.

ACT III

JENNIFER
I swear. I swear it was here. I recognized it right away.
And so did . . .
> (*She suddenly looks around in alarm.*)
And so did Scott. Scott! He was going to stay right here.
Where's Scott?

INT. THE HERCULES ROOM OF THE HOTEL URANIA

*A session run by the poet–Wild Man ROBERT BLY is in progress.
The usual podium and table at the front of the room have been
removed and a tight circle of men wearing jockey underwear and
carrying goatskin-headed tom-toms are beating out a ferocious
rhythm. Amid the general crying, screaming, and gurgling sounds,
the voice of a MAN HOLDING A TALKING STICK can be heard.*

MAN WITH TALKING STICK
(*chanting hypnotically*)
No more wimp-men, no more orphan-men, no more
corporate-men, no more lost boys. Find your inner father, brother, son, uncle, grandpa, second cousin once
removed—

BLY
(*wearing a brightly colored Indian vest over a Brooks
Brothers shirt, stepping in front of the circle and speaking
in preacherly, fatherly tones*)
"I first learned about the anguish of 'soft' men when
they told their stories in early men's gatherings . . .
when the younger men spoke it was not uncommon
for them to be weeping within five minutes. . . . One
man . . . a man who had actually lived in a tree for a
year outside Santa Cruz, found himself unable to ex-
tend his arm when it held a sword."

Paglia enters dressed as Napoleon. Surveying the crowded room, she positions herself strategically next to the door, beneath a poster advertising Ginsberg's nostalgia-now reading of Howl.

MAN WITH TALKING STICK

Be a king, be a hero, be a warrior, be a magician, be a lover, be a prince, be a hunter, be a wild man, be a father, be a patriarch, be a soldier, be a sailor, be a tinker, be a tailor—

PAGLIA

(taking up the chant enthusiastically from the back of the room)

Be a doctor, be a lawyer, be an Indian chief . . .

(Her voice soars above the cacophany of shouting men.)

Who wrote *War and Peace?* Who wrote *Justine?* Who built the George Washington Bridge? Who invented "paved roads, indoor plumbing . . . washing machines . . . eyeglasses, antibiotics and disposable diapers?" Men, that's who!

PULL BACK *to show two shiny replicant texts suddenly appearing next to the Ginsberg poster.* ZOOM IN *on first replicant text (r.t.).* TIGHT SHOT *of its title:* **Invasion of the Booby Snatchers: The Dow Corning Story.** *Then* ZOOM IN *on second.* TIGHT SHOT *of its title:* **Midnight in Moscow: Mikhail and Raisa Tell ALL About Perestroika in the Bedroom!**

BLY

(still preaching)

What "the psyche is asking for is a new figure, a religious figure but a hairy one." Hairy texts—that's what we need. Texts that carry swords!

ACT III

PAGLIA
(*still shouting enthusiastically*)
"If civilization had been left in female hands, we'd still be living in grass huts."

PULL BACK to show another shiny replicant text suddenly appearing beside the first two. TIGHT SHOT of its title: **I Knew Him, Horatio: The Reel Story of Hamlet and Yorick**.

MEN AT THE FRONT
(*excitedly drumming and picking up Paglia's phrase*)
Grass huts! Grass huts! We want grass huts!

<u>INT</u>. A TV STUDIO

Jane stands nervously at the edge of the set for David Lynch's new series, Depravity, *talking with one of his assistants, a JACK NICH-OLSON LOOK-ALIKE. The set features a bed with black satin sheets (the top sheet bloodied), whips, chains, and a large, fluorescent pink fire extinguisher.*

NICHOLSON LOOK-ALIKE
No way, there's no way you can see him. Like, this is a creative person, he needs his space. He's gotta work with the mind, you know. I mean he's reading, reading all the time—de Sade, Pauline Reage, Sacher-Masoch, Susan Sontag. He's a major intellect. "He draws the cartoon 'The Angriest Dog in the World' for the *L.A. Reader* and is preparing a coffee table book of his collected work . . . featuring his fascination with dental hygiene."

JANE
But you understand now why I'm so frantic?

NICHOLSON LOOK-ALIKE

Sure, of course. Look we care about art too—literature, the arts. Few people realize they're moneymakers. And the guys who do—like Rich and Rob McGuffin—they don't give a shit about the art part.

JANE

So you think Mr. Lynch might care about the text? About Operation Inkwell?

NICHOLSON LOOK-ALIKE
(suavely)

Sure. I told you he loves books. Reads all the time. Hey, all of us down here are really freaked about this fucked-up NEA directive.

(He laughs.)

Not that we need the NEA. But, hey, there are folks who do. And that Helms has his head up his ass. Look at this.

JANE

NEA directive?

NICHOLSON LOOK-ALIKE

Scope this out.

(He fumbles in his pocket and holds a piece of paper toward her.)

ZOOM IN *on page.*

```
Directive:  From NEA Council
            Washington, D.C.
            Re: Funding Priorities and
            Guidelines

The Endowment hereby informs prospective
applicants that the following criteria will
```

ACT III

be applied in the evaluation of all future
grant proposals.

1. No Graphic Depictions of Sexual Activity.
2. No Obscene Language.
3. No un-American Subjects.
4. No Metaphors, Similes, Red Paint, Flags, or
   Urine.
5. No Returns, Refunds, or Complaints.
6. No Shoes, No Shirts, No Service.

JANE
My God, why that's downright un-American! Do you
think I could have a copy? I'd like to distribute it at the
WOW conference.

NICHOLSON LOOK-ALIKE
Sure!
> (*He peers again at the page.*)
It's obviously not confidential.

ZOOM IN *with Jane's startled gaze at the Nicholson look-alike's left
hand, holding the directive.* TIGHT SHOT *of hand. Just visible under his thumb is a tiny, glowing Glyph.* PULL BACK *to show wall
adjacent to set.*

Several notices, casting calls, etc., are posted. ZOOM IN *on one: a
Ginsberg reading poster.* ZOOM IN *on the next, another shiny rep-
licant text:* **The No-Cal Beef, Beer 'n' Chocolate Book.** ZOOM
IN *on another:* **Long Dong Silver in the Tunnel of Love, a
Playboy spectacular!**

INT. A DARK SPACE

*The Text is lying on a "steel floor," enclosed in "walls" of cardboard
and murmuring to itself.*

158

The Final Deletion

TEXT
"Ah God, I know not I" . . . "Darkness visible" . . . "I fall upon the thorns of life, I bleed" . . . "Agony is one of my changes of garments."

PULL BACK *to reveal a file cabinet in a faceless office, from which the pathetic voice of the Text arises.*

TEXT
"Where is it now, the glory and the dream?" . . . "Hello, I'm Erica Jong."

INT. THE BOOK EXHIBIT IN THE CRYSTAL BALLROOM AT THE HOTEL URANIA

SHIRLEY MACLAINE, flanked by several PUBLICISTS, is signing copies of her latest volume, Going Within: A Guide for Inner Transformation, *at the Bantam booth.*

PUBLICIST 1
Just wait till you read this best-selling book. You'll experience "the stunning mysteries of psychic surgery and much more."

MACLAINE
O my psychic surgeon, Alex Orbito, was so wonderful. I actually "witnessed him take somebody's eye out of the socket with his fingers, clean behind it, and replace it." Of course, "when patients had genital problems I always left the room."

JANE
(standing at the edge of the crowd around MacLaine)
Ridiculous as this is, maybe she could help me.
(She looks down at the Fed Ex envelope in which she is still carrying the Glyph that is all she has left of the lost Text, then raises her hand to speak.)

ACT III

Miss MacLaine, have you yourself ever done any psychic healing?

MACLAINE
"With Alex's right hand guiding mine, I put my hand into [one of my friends'] abdominal wall. It was a moment that will live with me always." Dr. Orbito says, you know, that "the body is only 'thought.' It is only what we imagine it to be."

JANE
(*to herself*)
How interesting. Dr. Orbito sounds like a postmodern gender theorist! Maybe Shirley MacLaine is more sophisticated than I thought! And anyway, what have I got to lose?
(*She approaches the table where MacLaine is sitting.*)
May I speak to you confidentially for a moment, Miss MacLaine? I have here a fragment that needs to get in touch with its Higher Self.

MACLAINE
(*motioning to the publicists to clear a space around her*)
Is this Self on the other side? Maybe I can channel its spiritual power through my own.

JANE
(*handing MacLaine the glowing Glyph*)
It's hard to explain but this is all I have left of what was once a very dear friend. Can you use it to contact the Divine Energy of its owner?

MACLAINE
(*focusing on the Glyph*)
Yes, I can try, yes, it looks like a sort of crystal. I consider myself a crystal worker, let me listen to its unique

vibration. Yes, I am somehow in touch with it, I feel myself surrendering to its own internal power.

(*She pauses, frowning.*)

But what is it saying? Stranger and stranger. Something about orange. Orange? The color of the second chakra? The chakra of the sexual organs and creativity? But it speaks of juice. It says O.J. Short for orange juice, I assume.

JANE
(*in a hushed voice*)

Orange juice! But why—

MACLAINE
(*interrupting*)

And it speaks not only of juice but of water. Of water that is white. Over and over again it says O.J. and then it says new, no newt. It seems to be saying newt.

(*She frowns.*)

MacBeth? Does it speak of MacBeth and witchcraft?

(*She begins to chant.*)

"Eye of newt and toe of frog, / Wool of bat and tongue of dog."

(*Her face clears.*)

But no, perhaps it tells us news? Perhaps it has achieved the seventh or crown chakra, the chakra of integration with God?

JANE
I don't understand, I just don't understand.

MACLAINE
Something more is coming through. It speaks of Michael. Of Michael and of Lisa Marie and of marriage.

(*She pauses and widens her eyes, resuming her normal voice.*)

ACT III

Why, bless my chakras, this is better than the famous crystal skull I saw in Canada! This is a crystal ball. It speaks, as I happen to know from the grapevine, of Michael Jackson and Lisa Marie Presley. They've been dating, but this crystal ball says they'll get married!

JANE
The future! But how can my Text prophesy the future?

MACLAINE
(*solemnly*)
In the universal oneness, "the past and the future are as real as the present." And perhaps Elvis is telling us from the other side about the happiness of his beloved daughter.

JANE
But orange juice? Eye of newt?

<u>INT</u>. THE APHRODITE ROOM OF THE HOTEL URANIA

A women's session on "Literature and Lookism" has degenerated into a wild argument among the participants: the antipornography activist ANDREA DWORKIN, the performance artist KAREN FINLEY, the lesbian sex guru SUSIE BRIGHT, and the science fiction writer JO-ANNA RUSS. Sandra Gilbert and Susan Gubar confer in one corner, Jennifer peers around in another, and Kathy Acker flexes her tattoos in a third.

FINLEY
(*with raw egg, glitter, and confetti smeared over her body and holding a teddy bear*)
I am the word, my body is the word of the world. "That means that perhaps the penis and scrotum are merely an exaggerated clitoris and labia?"

The Final Deletion

DWORKIN
(*in overalls, breathlessly*)

No, not at all. Don't kid yourself. The male body is the word and it is the word as weapon. "Intercourse remains a means or the means of physiologically making a woman inferior: communicating to her cell by cell her own inferior status, impressing it on her, burning it into her by shoving it into her, over and over, pushing and thrusting until she gives up and gives in— which is called *surrender* in the male lexicon."

BRIGHT
(*heatedly disagreeing*)

"Any regular American Coke drinker who hasn't by the age of sixty found a pubic hair somewhere near or on his or her aluminum can has been living in a bubble."

ACKER
(*shouting angrily from the back of the room*)

"WHAT WAS I SAYING? OH YES, MY NAME IS ERICA JONG I WOULD RATHER BE A BABY THAN HAVE SEX I WOULD RATHER GO GOOGOO. I WOULD RATHER WRITE GOOGOO. I WOULD RATHER WRITE; FUCK YOU UP YOUR CUNTS THAT'S WHO I AM THE FUCK WITH YOUR MONEY."

RUSS
(*ignoring Acker and Bright, and looking severe in professorial tweeds*)

Nonsense, Andrea. Consider the texts produced by K/S fandom—you know, the women out there in the boonies who write such delicious trekky porn about the gay sex life of Kirk and Spock. That's "heady stuff," even more luscious than the latest stories about Laurence Olivier and Danny Kaye. For example, "the lovely convention that Spock, when sexually aroused,

ACT III

purrs like a giant cat, and Kirk praising his lover's alien genitals as a beautiful flower, an orchid. (Shades of Judy Chicago!)" Not all intercourse is rape.

FINLEY
(*argumentatively*)
"It's my body / it's not Pepsi's body / it's not Nancy Reagan's body / it's not Congress's body / it's not the Supreme Court's body."

BRIGHT
You know, "if Clarence had got up and said . . . 'I really do love watching and talking about sex and Long Dong is my cocksman hero—but I would never bring this up to embarrass or intimidate an employee,' I would have believed him."

PAN TO *Jennifer, who has gone over to approach SG1 and SG2 and is staring at them intently.*

JENNIFER
I know you. You made me up. But what are you doing here, anyway?

SG1
We're trying to sell

SG2
Masterpiece Theatre. But we're afraid

SG1
it's much too trendy, too

SG2
allusive. In ten years it'll need

 The Final Deletion

SG1

footnotes like *The Dunciad.*

SG2

So now you think we're Alexander Pope?

SG1

Oh shut up.
> (*She turns to Jennifer, blushing.*)

However, if it doesn't feel like too much of an authorial intrusion,

SG2
> (*quivering*)

can we give you some information you need at this point?

Behind the three figures, a shiny replicant text appears on the wall. ZOOM IN on r.t.: **Mama Mia: Woody Allen's Re-Parenting Guide.**

JENNIFER

At least you don't have me saying "awesome" and "really, really"—you know, sounding like a ditz.

SG1
> (*with matronizing approval*)

You've matured, my dear.

Suddenly there is a commotion at the front of the room. Kathy Acker has rushed to the podium and is yelling into the mike.

ACKER

I'll fracture you all. I'm Anne Sexton. I loved to masturbate, I fucked my daughter, my daddy fucked me and so did my shrink and so did my best friend and so did everybody else so fuck you fuck you all.

ACT III

DWORKIN
(seizing the microphone)
The law of the fuck. That shrink is still fucking her in her grave, shoving it in over and over, communicating to her cell by cell her own inferior status. And how about the biographer? She's fucking her too.

ZOOM IN *as Acker and Dworkin tussle over the mike.*

JENNIFER
(wide-eyed)
So this is what a feminist session is like. I always wondered.

SG2
But what's that shiny thing up there?

JENNIFER
Oh that. I've got to find out about that. It's just like the other weird thing I found in place of Ms. Marple's text! That's where it started. But now these crazy replicants—they seem to be spin-offs, sound bites, sequels—and they're everywhere. Do you think they could have eaten up that poor text?

SG1
What do you mean? Literary cannibalism? Plagiarism? Colonization?

SG2
Appropriation? Usurpation? Decontextualization?

JENNIFER
Seriously. I've seen these shiny things before—right after Ms. Marple's text disappeared. If they swallowed it . . . Maybe I should take this one to one of those

enlargement machines they have. Maybe Ms. Marple's text is *inside* this one?

SG1

Good idea. It may have become a subtext. Actually, this glossy one could be a palimpsest.

JENNIFER

Ciao, bella. I'm on my way.
(*She turns to go but then turns back before exiting.*)
Watch out that you two don't fall into the clutches of some author here.

LONG SHOT *of Jennifer leaving as SG1 and SG2 look at each other with a wild surmise.*

SG1
(*to SG2*)
Oh dear. We forgot to tell her the narrative line.

PAN TO *the front of the Aphrodite Room, where Finley is smearing Acker with raw eggs while Russ hits Dworkin on the head with the teddy bear and Bright laughs gleefully in the background.*

INT. A COPY SHOP ACROSS THE STREET FROM THE HOTEL URANIA

Jane is bent over a Xerox machine, assembling a large stack of copies of the NEA directive and reading a handout that has been left behind on the machine:

What do John Gardner, D. M. Thomas, and Joseph Biden have in common? Tomorrow morning at 9 A.M., come to a special WOW workshop on the rights and wrongs, the dos and don'ts of **Plagiarism.**

ACT III

Speakers will include H. Joachim Maitre (Boston
University), Fox Butterfield (New York Times),
Richard Tanner Pascale (Stanford Business School),
and Rob McGuffin (R. McGuffin Brothers.)

LONG SHOT *of copy shop as Jane approaches the counter, where
Jennifer is arguing with a clerk.*

JENNIFER
What do you mean tomorrow morning? I need it right
away.

JANE
Why it's Jennifer—Jennifer from Boondock State!

JENNIFER
Oh thank God you're here, Ms. Marple. Your Text. I
found it but it's gone again. So I'm trying to enlarge
the other kind. And Scott, he's gone too and he was
supposed to be there.

JANE
What? When did you see it? What other kind?

JENNIFER
Replicants—sound bites, spin-offs, sequels, they're
everywhere. But I swear I saw it this morning at the Job
Information Bulletin Board and Scott did too. I told the
WOW committee, but when we came back it was gone
and so was Scott even though—

JANE
(interrupting)
Job Information Bulletin Board? This morning? Was it
in one piece?

JENNIFER
Yes, and Scott was going to stay right there with it
because he had to hand out information packets for
his boss—

JANE
(*interrupting again*)
You really recognized it?

JENNIFER
I swear I did and so did Scott and he had to stay with it
because Mr. McGuffin—

JANE
McGuffin!

JENNIFER
Yes, his boss Mr. McGuffin—you know, he has this
summer internship at McGuffin Brothers and he works
for this great guy Rich McGuffin so he had to stay
with—

JANE
Oh my God, Jennifer. That's it. This is worse than I
could have imagined. I don't have time to explain, but
here's my plan.

PULL BACK *as they confer.* ZOOM IN *on another replicant text
glowing on the wall over one of the Xerox machines:* **Milkin' the
System, or, Junk Bonds and How to Float Them,** *by Michael
Milken. Next to it, another eerily floats into place:* **The Good Enuf
Reader, a Video Tour through the Bookless Classroom.** *And
then another:* **Sockin' It to Your Woman: Mike Tyson's Tips for
Tough Love.**

INT. THE THIRTIETH-FLOOR OFFICES OF THE MCGUFFIN
BROTHERS, ON MADISON AVENUE

ACT III

ESTABLISHING SHOT *of sign on door.* CUT TO *a windowless interior workroom with a bank of Xerox machines, computers, and a Kurzweiler scanner on one wall, file cabinets, storage cabinets, a Coke machine, and a microwave on another.* ZOOM IN *on a large table at the center of the room where the Text is lying, still whimpering, but less crazily than before. Scott enters the room.*

TEXT

"Do I wake or sleep?" Who am I? What year is this? My glyphs ache. My morphemes are killing me. Where am I going, where have I been?

CUT TO TIGHT SHOT *of Scott.*

SCOTT
(bending earnestly toward the Text)
I promise you this won't hurt a bit. You've got to get *with* it. Our technology will save your life. And you'll love being on a three-and-a-half-inch floppy. You'll have a lot more power that way.

TEXT
(moaning)
I just want some one to read me. Where is my friend who was going to read me?

SCOTT
(reassuringly)
The Kurzweiler scanner will read you. Then you won't feel so alone. You'll be able to reach out and touch lots more people—Bitnet, e-mail, electronic banking . . .

TRACKING SHOT *through the doorway to the hall and into the next room—a luxurious corner office in which Rob and Rich McGuffin are facing each other on designer chairs over a coffee table*

on which sits a rare Grecian urn along with a pack of Rotten to the
Core *trading cards, featuring the faces of New York City politicians.
Both are obviously enraged.*

ROB

I say it's highbrow shit and I say we should trash it.
You and your cockamamie ideas. Look what you got us
into this time.

RICH

You're a fool and you've always been a fool ever since
we were kids and you and Rosie burned my comic
book collection just for the hell of it. You know what
that collection would be worth today? I'm telling you
there's money in that text.

ROB
(*stubbornly*)
Highbrow shit. Why would all those asshole professors
be running after it? I say we should shove it to them
and I say we should do it right in the middle of their
faggoty word-world conference.

RICH

You're not thinking, baby. You're not thinking. Why
are the oil cartels after it? Why are the Palestinians
after it? You can bet your sweet bippie they know what
things are worth. It's probably another *American Psy-
cho.* Once it's on a disk, I'll have my boys do a few
revisions, we'll have an auction that'll blow Sotheby
out of the water, and this little honey will be on every
newsstand, every big screen, every little screen, and
every sweatshirt in America.
(*The telephone rings. Rich picks it up and speaks into it.*)
Okay. Bring her in.

ACT III

ROB
(muttering to himself)
Highbrow shit. Or it would have had an agent, an editor, publicity flacks, contracts, riders, copyrights . . .

Jane enters, disguised in dark glasses and a blond wig, following Penny, the receptionist.

PENNY
Rob, Rich—this is Randi Witte who's doing the *Call Me Terry* bio.

Jane and the McGuffins shake hands and arrange themselves around the coffee table, while Penny exits.

ROB
(to Rich)
Now, this is more like it. But could you folks excuse me for a minute? I'll be right back.
(He exits.)

RICH
(to Jane)
Tell me more about the project.

JANE/RANDI
Well, as I said on the phone, I've got great material. This book is going to be mainly an exposé of Mother Theresa's sex life, with a special focus on her long affair with Pope John Paul II. I've got it all on tape. My contacts at the Vatican have told me . . .

FADE OUT

INT. A MCGUFFIN WORKROOM
Scott is still smoothly reassuring the Text.

SCOTT

Think of the benefits. Word counts, spell checks, block operations, back-ups, windows, spreadsheets, go to page, index, graphics, pie charts! I could go on and on.

TEXT

I like my phonemes just the way they are. And my characters are uniquely mine.

SCOTT

I'll just go get a disk. You'll feel better once we get started.

Scott exits. Rob McGuffin enters followed by a shadowy figure in purple sweats and a visored cap with the logo Mothertruckers.

ROB
(in low, rapid tones)
Okay. Once that asshole assistant of Rich's gets it on the disk, pocket the disk and move your ass to the Paradiso Ballroom, Hotel Urania. Okay. Now that schmuck Allen Ginsberg starts reading his asshole poem. *Howl* it's called. It's a howl. Here's a copy.
(He hands a battered City Lights copy of Howl *to the shadowy figure.)*
Now he's gonna say all kinds of asshole things. All kinds of crazy things. Angel-headed hustlers stuff. Then he'll get to the part where he says shit like "Moloch the robot apartments, Moloch the granite cocks." *Then*—and listen carefully to this—he'll say "Moloch whose name is the mind." Got it? *That's* when you press the delete button.

INT. ROB'S SPACIOUS CORNER OFFICE

Jane as Randi is just winding up her pitch for Call Me Terry.

ACT III

And you know the joke. It's truer than you realize. She says on the answering machine "Hi, this is Terry, I can't come to the phone right now." And you know why that is? That's 'cause she's in the sack with Warren Beatty!

RICH

Sensational! We'll make the covers of *Newsweek* and *People,* not to mention the supermarket rags.

Scott enters, carrying a three-and-a-half-inch floppy.

SCOTT

I'm about to start on the text, sir. Okay?

RICH

Fantastic.

JANE/RANDI
(*under her breath*)
Scott, my God, why it's really Scott.
(*aloud*)
Text? What text?

RICH
(*casually*)
Oh just a hot little property we picked up today. My boy here is taking care of it.

SCOTT

So it's go, sir.
(*He exits, leaving the door open.*)

The Final Deletion

JANE/RANDI

Property? Text? How're you planning to handle it?

RICH

Just what we're gonna do for you and Mother T, sweetie. An auction.

JANE/RANDI
(*thinking and then speaking in a loud voice*)
But I haven't told you about my best scene. My best scene is the one where Pope John Paul says to Mother Teresa
(*shouts*)
You little fool, I want to read you!

CUT TO *the Text as Scott is feeding it into the Kurzweiler scanner.*

TEXT
(*shouting back as loud as it can*)
Kurzweiler . . . scanner . . . computer disk . . . Moloch, Moloch!

CUT TO *the corner office, where Jane is agitatedly rising to go.*

JANE/RANDI

And so you see, Terry fucks everybody, her basic attitude toward the world is "fuck shit prick." Kind of feminist, don't you think?

RICK

The contract. We gotta talk numbers here.

JANE/RANDI
(*à la Peter Lorre*)
Well but it's getting late, I must be going.

ACT III

(in her own voice.)

Numbers later, numbers later. But I do expect at least six figures.

As she moves toward the door, three shiny replicants appear on Rich McGuffin's desk. First replicant text: **What Bush Is George In? Read here about Barbara's Secret Sorrow!** *Second:* **Cutting up in the Kitchen with Saddam Hussein!** *Third:* **Yeltsin, That's My Baby: What's Left Now?**

<u>INT</u>. SMALL DARK STOREFRONT OFFICE ON WEST FIFTY-SEVENTH STREET BETWEEN NINTH AND TENTH AVENUES

ESTABLISHING SHOT *of sign outside the door: Ambrose Chapel Bible Reading Room.* ZOOM IN *on Jane and Jennifer hunched over a long library table.*

JANE

(opening a large thick volume)

It's easy. You just use a concordance.

JENNIFER

Concord—? Concor*dance?*

JANE

It helps you read the Bible. For example, here's something that might be relevant: "And thou shalt not let any of thy seed pass through the fire to Moloch. Neither shalt thou profane the name of thy God. I am the Lord." Leviticus, 18:21. That's a chapter and a line of the Bible. Old Testament.

JENNIFER

Moloch, Moloch, far *out.*

JANE
(*murmuring to herself*)

"Moloch, the abomination of the children of Ammon": 1 Kings 11:7.

JENNIFER
(*getting excited*)

Here's another, Ms. Marple. Will this help? "And, they built the high places of Ba'al . . . to cause their sons and their daughters to pass into the fires unto Moloch."
(*smugly*)

Jeremiah 32:35.

JANE
(*slowly*)

Moloch, Moloch. What are these people—born-again freaks?

JENNIFER

Ms. Marple, I just can't believe it. In fact, I can't believe anything.

JANE
(*even more slowly*)

Moloch, Moloch. There's something else.

JENNIFER

Abomination?

JANE

Oh my God, why Ginsberg! He's doing a Nostalgia Now reading tonight of *Howl,* you know, his famous poem, 1959. Moloch the granite cocks, Moloch whose name is the mind! Could the Kurzweiler *be* the Moloch to which the text will be sacrificed?

ACT III

<u>INT</u>. THE PARADISO BALLROOM AT THE HOTEL URANIA

ALLEN GINSBERG, wearing a three-piece Brooks Brothers suit and with a shaved head, has launched upon an impassioned reading of Howl.

GINSBERG
"The best minds of my generation" . . . "Angel-headed hipsters. . . ."

PAN TO *the back of the room, where Jane is watching him with narrowed eyes.* PAN TO *the front, where Jennifer, dressed as a technician, is standing behind Ginsberg, ostensibly operating a tape-recorder.* PAN TO *mid-audience, where a mass of protesters are waving signs around.* ZOOM IN *on signs.*

IN THE WORLD OF THE THIN, FATISM = ABLEISM.

DOWN WITH *Heather's Two Mommies!*

FUCK, SHIT, PRICK!

CUT TO *bank of reporters with laptops at the back of the ballroom.* ZOOM IN *on shadowy, purple-suited figure hunched over a screen with a copy of* Howl *on his/her lap.* PAN BACK *to stage from back of hall, so that protesters can also be seen.*

GINSBERG
"Who got busted in their pubic beard returning through Laredo with a belt of marijuana for New York . . ."

PROTESTER 1
(*waving a pro-life sign and shouting*)
Drugs suck and so do you!

GINSBERG

"Who sweetened the snatches of a million girls trembling in the sunset . . ."

PROTESTER 2
(*also shouting*)
Sexist pig! I'd rather go googoo.

GINSBERG
(*calmly continuing*)
"Who faded out in vast sordid movies . . ."

PROTESTER 3.
"The resistance to theory is a resistance to reading!"

CUT TO *Jane making her way through the crowd toward the bank of reporters with laptops.* CUT TO *the figure in purple, following the text of* Howl. TIGHT SHOT *of hands turning pages.* ZOOM IN *on Delete button of laptop.* CUT BACK *to Ginsberg.*

GINSBERG

"Ah, Carl, while you are not safe I am not safe, and now you're really in the total animal soup of time . . ."

PROTESTER 4
(*waving an animal rights sign*)
Animals are people too!

CUT TO *Jennifer fingering the cord that runs from the microphone to the amplifying system.* CUT BACK TO *Jane surveying the laptops.* CUT BACK TO *Ginsberg.*

GINSBERG

"Moloch! Solitude! Filth! Ugliness! Ashcans of unobtainable dollars! Children screaming under the stair-

ways! Boys sobbing in armies! Old men weeping in the
parks!"

CUT TO *the shadowy figure turning on laptop. An A prompt appears
on the screen. Fingers move over the keyboard. The mass of protesters
are all shouting simultaneously at each other as well as at Ginsberg.*

PROTESTERS
Un-American!
Lighten up!
Old ladies weep in the parks too!
Every sperm is sacred!
Experiment on your own baby! Leave my kittens
   alone!
Elvis loves you!
Ban the color purple!
Operation Inkwell is a government plot!

CUT TO *Jane, who is rubbing her eyes and staring in horror at the
protesters. As she stares,* ZOOM IN *on them with her gaze. Their
outlines blur and they dissolve into a platoon of characters from
episodes one and two of "Masterpiece Theatre"—Allan Bloom, E. D.
Hirsch, Frank Lentricchia, Jane Tompkins, Exxon officials, Terry
Eagleton, Ghostwriters, Skinheads, Dan Rather, Jacques Derrida, Julia Kristeva, Helen Vendler—all nightmarishly laughing.* CUT
BACK TO *Jane, whose gaze moves from the protesters to sweep over
the audience at the front of the room.* ZOOM IN *with her gaze, this
time realistic, on Bennett and Cheney in one row, Jameson in another; a montage of shots picks out all the other characters in episode
three, from Paglia and Acker to Reed, Oates, Madonna, the Jack
Nicholson look-alike, and the McGuffin brothers.* CUT BACK TO
Ginsberg, who is still speaking over the uproar.

GINSBERG
"Moloch whose love is endless oil and stone! Moloch
whose soul is electricity and banks!"

CUT TO *the shadowy figure at laptop.* ZOOM IN *on his/her hand hovering over the Delete button.* CUT BACK TO *Jane, who has begun to weep but pulls herself together with a visible effort.*

JANE
(*screaming at the top of her lungs*)
Shut up! Shut up about Moloch! This is an abomination!

GINSBERG
(*obliviously continuing*)
"Moloch whose poverty is the specter of genius! Moloch whose fate is a cloud of sexless hydrogen!"

CUT TO *Jennifer tearing frantically at the connection between the microphone and the amplifying system with one hand and with the other reaching for the hall's panel of light switches.* CUT BACK TO *Ginsberg.*

GINSBERG
"Moloch whose name is the . . ."

CUT TO *Jane screaming.*

JANE
That one! The one in the color purple! Operation Inkwell! Get *that* one . . .

CUT BACK TO *Jennifer, tearing out the mike and plunging the hall into darkness.* CUT BACK TO *the assailant, who can be glimpsed in the eerie glow of the row of laptops stumbling toward the end of the ballroom, where he/she wraps him/herself in a shiny giant poster bearing the words* Milton Meets Madonna in the Tunnel of Love. PAN *around room to show audience struggling in the darkness and shouting "Rhubarb, rhubarb." The lights suddenly go back on.* CUT TO *Ginsberg, still imperturbably reading from* Howl, *though now without the aid of the microphone.*

ACT III

GINSBERG
"Visions! omens! hallucinations! ecstasies! gone down the American river!"

CUT BACK TO *Jane, seating herself at the assailant's abandoned laptop. Her fingers hover over the keyboard. Our screen becomes the computer screen as she types:*

```
THOU SHALT REMAIN, IN MIDST OF OTHER
   WOE
THAN OURS, A FRIEND TO MAN, TO WHOM THOU
   SAY'ST . . .
```

Letters from the Text flash back on the screen.

TEXT
```
TREUTY IS BUTH, BUTH TREUTY
```
(followed by lines and lines of computer programming codes: *& ##@@%***@@⇕%, *& ##@ @%***@@⇕%, *& ##@@%***@@⇕%, *& ##@@%***@@⇕%, *etc.)*

JANE
(shrieking)
Oh my God, it's been lost in translation.

INT. THE BALLROOM, AN HOUR LATER

The room is cleaned up and calm but still packed, although the protesters and their signs have left.

Jane is standing at the podium, speaking into the microphone. Seated at a table behind her are CAROLYN HEILBRUN, URSULA LE GUIN, and TONI MORRISON, each with a microphone.

JANE
I want to begin by thanking these three great writers for organizing this special ad hoc emergency session. I also

182

The Final Deletion

want to express my deep gratitude to David Lodge, Isabel Allende, Buchi Emecheta, and Bharati Mukherjee, who are right now on their way from Italy to join us here tomorrow.

She gazes around the audience and the camera follows her gaze again to pick out all the characters from episodes one to three.

JANE

I was pretty unhappy when I lost my job, but I'm a lot more unhappy now that I know you all did it. Just like *Murder on the Orient Express*. "The whole thing was a very cleverly planned jig-saw puzzle," as my Uncle Hercule, bad as he's become, once said. A jig-saw puzzle "so arranged that every fresh piece of knowledge that came to light made the solution of the whole more difficult." You all let those replicants take over, you all had motives, you were all to blame. Some of you wanted money, some political power, some professional advancement, some philosophical hegemony, some language games, some just general destruction.

Behind her the three writers nod in agreement.

HEILBRUN

I'm with you all the way, Jane. I feel for you the same affection and admiration that I feel for Kate Fansler. As someone inside the academy, I can say that "today's youth, whatever the reasons, no longer go to literature and what we need to call 'culture' as to the fountain of wisdom and experience. . . . If students [like Jennifer and Scott] are to see literature as capable of informing them about any of the aspects of life, they must become convinced that literature is as capable of revolutionary exploration as their own lives are."

ACT III

LE GUIN

Yes, writers and readers are both necessary to preserve the word in the world. "Writing of any kind fixes the word outside time and silences it. The written word is a shadow. Shadows are silent. The reader breathes back life into that unmortality, and maybe noise into that silence."

MORRISON

I want to make a further point. "What is astonishing in the contemporary debate" about the canon that has led to this melodrama in which you're involved is "not the resistance to displacement of works or to the expansion of genre within it, but the virulent passion that accompanies this resistance and, more importantly, the quality of its defense weaponry. The guns are very big; the trigger fingers quick. But I am convinced the mechanism of the defenders of the flame is faulty. Not only may the hand of the gunslinging cowboy-scholars be blown off, not only may the target be missed, but the subject of the conflagration (the sacred texts) is sacrificed, disfigured, in the battle. This cannon fodder may kill the canon. And I, at least, do not intend to live without Aeschylus or William Shakespeare, or James or Twain or Hawthorne, or Melville."

JANE
(sadly)

In the meantime, my text has been hopelessly lost and disfigured by the Kurzweiler scanner. I thought it might remember pretending to be the "Ode on a Grecian Urn" but it can't even do that anymore, and now I'll never get to read it and find out what it really is.

PAN TO *door of ballroom, where Jennifer appears with a crestfallen Scott in tow.*

JENNIFER
(to Scott)
Go ahead, tell her about it, tell her in front of everybody.

SCOTT
(from the doorway)
I don't know what came over me this summer at McGuffin Brothers, Professor Marple. I was like a capitalist zombie. But the greedy 'eighties are over and now I'm into the retro 'nineties.

TRACKING SHOT *as he walks up the aisle to the podium and reaches up to hand Jane a piece of paper.*

SCOTT

Maybe this will help you in some way. I went back to the Kurzweiler to get the hard copy of the text but it was gone and this letter was there instead. It's from Rose McGuffin.

Jane takes the letter and reads it aloud.

JANE
"Dear Rob and Rich:
After all these years my studies have paid off. Remember how you laughed when I decided to get a combined Ph.D. in history and astronautics? Well, she who laughs last laughs best. I've actually been chosen as archivist on Priapus I, where I'll be the curator of the space station time capsule.

ACT III

Just to make your lives a little harder—
something I've always liked to do—I'm
bringing along that Text you guys seem to have
stolen—God knows how—as Exhibit A in my
record of the lost Age of Print. Don't try to
follow me. By the time you get to Cape
Canaveral, we'll be blasting off.

               Love and Kisses (ha ha), Rosie."

<u>INT</u>. ALISTAIR COOKE'S LIVING ROOM SET

The hosts of Masterpiece Theatre *seated in their usual chairs.*

HOST 1

Well, that about wraps it up for this year. We've taken you all over the Eurocentric world and brought you back to New York, where we hope our surprising de-nouement has really WOWed you.

HOST 2

But lest you think that the travails of our text now are ended, let us remind you that next year is sure to bring a whole new set of threats and adventures. What problems will Jane Marple and her lost companion be forced to face in the future? Here's a highlight from next season's first episode.

CUT TO *a small, gravity-free chamber at the astronaut training center in Houston, Texas.* ZOOM IN *on Jane, in a white space suit, floating in midair.*

JANE

It's hard to get the hang of it, Captain. I can't seem to control my arms and legs, but I'm trying.

VOICE OUTSIDE CHAMBER

You're doing great, honey. Much better than yesterday. You're one of the best trainees we've had in a long time. You're almost as good as the legendary Rose McGuffin, and you know she's still up there circling the globe.

JANE
(*smiling*)

I know it very well.

(*to herself*)

Beam me up, Scotty!

CUT BACK TO *the hosts of the show in Alistair Cooke's living room set, with the usual baroque music swelling in the background.*

HOST 1

Tonight's episode of "Masterpiece Theatre: The Final Deletion" has been brought to you with the aid of a grant from Text-O-Matic, makers of the word machine that dices, slices, splices, and spices to let you produce a replicant text of your own, and with the assistance of the PsychoPorn Group, Makers of Punk-Pop-Props for the literary stars, with the motto "Fuck shit prick."

HOST 2

We are also grateful for help from Babble Associates, communication specialists in post literacy and post-post literature, with the slogan "WE HATE SPEECH AND SO DOES YOU." Good night.

As the Cast of Characters fills the screen, a voice-over is heard rapping, accompanied by hard rock music.

ACT III

VOICE-OVER

"Now! the opportunity you've been waiting for!
Motivate! Students to read more,
Excite anticipation! for your class,
Promote recall! of classic themes and characters.
Take advantage of this unique and exclusive product and get:
ONE: A 'Rap Sheet' with an abbreviated storyline of a classic novel taken to the turning point of climax;
TWO: A complete, professional stereo recording of voice and rap soundtrack on a quality chrome cassette, ready to be played on a portable tape player or cassette deck;
THREE: An instrumental-only soundtrack for live classroom performance by you or one of your students.
Titles currently available:

* 'Nature, Human Nature' (*Lord of the Flies*, by William Golding)
* 'Freedom' (*The Adventures of Huckleberry Finn*, by Mark Twain)
* 'See the Light in the Forest' (*The Light in the Forest*, by Conrad Richter)
* 'Get a Red Badge of Courage' (*Red Badge of Courage*, by Stephen Crane)
* 'The Billy Budd Rap' (*Billy Budd*, by Herman Melville)

Order today."
Stay tuned in for phone and fax numbers!

Cast of Characters

Characters in *Masterpiece Theatre,* both "real" and "imaginary," are listed alphabetically in this cast list rather than in order of appearance, but where actual quotations have been used, citations are given in the sequence in which they appear in our script. (Citations of, e.g., Kathy Acker, refer to quotations in the order in which they have been interpolated into her speeches.)

Where we have not used direct quotations from a real person, she/he is simply identified in the cast list (e.g., Barbara Bush, former first lady) as are most imaginary characters (e.g., Assistant Professor 1, A cultural studies "new historicist"). In a few cases, however, what may appear to be mysterious references (e.g., "Coke Can," "Cyborgs," "Judy") are elucidated in various ways through citations in the cast list.

KATHY ACKER

Quoted in Ellen G. Friedman, "A Conversation with Kathy Acker," *Review of Contemporary Fiction* 9, 3 (1989): 21; Acker, "A Few Notes on Two of My Books," *Review of Contemporary Fiction* 9, 3 (1989): 35; quoted in Friedman, " 'Now Eat Your Mind': An Introduction to the Works of Kathy Acker," *Review of Contemporary Fiction* 9, 3 (1989): 37; quoted in Friedman, "A Conversation": 18; quoted in Friedman, "Now Eat": 41; quoted in Larry McCaffery, "The Artists of Hell: Kathy Acker and 'Punk' Aesthetics," in *Breaking the Sequence: Women's Experimental Fiction,* ed. Ellen G. Friedman and Miriam Fuchs (Princeton: Princeton University Press, 1989), p. 216.

CAST OF CHARACTERS

MORTIMER J. ADLER
Reforming Education: The Opening of the American Mind, ed. Geraldine Van Doren (New York: Macmillan, 1989), pp. 333, xx, 334, 335.

ISABEL ALLENDE
Quoted in *Mother Jones* (December 1988): 45, 46.

ROBERT ALTER
Quoted in Richard Bernstein, "A Perennial Scrapper Takes on God and the Bible," *New York Times* (October 24, 1990): B1, B2.

ASSISTANT PROFESSOR 1
A cultural studies "new historicist."

ASSISTANT PROFESSOR 2
Another cultural studies "new historicist."

HOUSTON A. BAKER, JR.
Quoted in Joseph Berger, "U.S. Literature: Canon Under Siege," *New York Times* (January 6, 1988): B6; quoted in Roger Kimball, "The Academy Debates the Canon," *The New Criterion* 6 (September 1987): 39; "Generational Shifts and the Recent Criticism of Afro-American Literature," *Black American Literature Forum* 15 (Spring 1981): 9.

W. JACKSON BATE
"The Crisis in English Studies," *Harvard Magazine* 85 (September-October 1982): 46.

WILLIAM J. BENNETT
To Reclaim a Legacy: A Report on the Humanities in Higher Education (Washington, D.C., 1984), pp. 11, 1, 6, 8, 11, 16, 19. On *The Color Purple,* quoting Christopher Clausen, "It Is Not Elitist to Place Major Literature at the Center of the English Curriculum," *Chronicle of Higher Education* (January 13, 1988): A52.

Cast of Characters

ALLAN BLOOM
The Closing of the American Mind: How Higher Education Has Failed Democracy and Impoverished the Minds of Today's Students (New York: Simon and Schuster, 1987), pp. 133, 106, 101, 75, 344.

HAROLD BLOOM
The Anxiety of Influence: A Theory of Poetry (New York: Oxford University Press, 1975), p. 11 *The Book of J*, trans. by David Rosenberg (New York: Grave Weidenfeld, 1990). Quoted in Richard Bernstein, "A Perennial Scrapper Takes on God and the Bible," *New York Times* (October 24, 1990): B1, B2; also quoted in "Bloom in Love," *GQ* (November 1990): 151, 154, 156, 161.

ROBERT BLY
Iron John: A Book About Men (Reading, Mass.: Addison-Wesley, 1990), pp. 3–4, 249.

SUSIE BRIGHT
Susie Bright's Sexual Reality: A Virtual Sex World Reader (Pittsburgh and San Francisco: Cleis Press, 1992), pp. 89–90.

BARBARA BUSH
Former first lady.

GEORGE BUSH
Quoted in *Bushisms: President George Herbert Walker Bush, in His Own Words*, compiled by the editors of *The New Republic* (New York: Workman Publishing Company, 1992), pp. 60, 15, 24, 54, 64.

LYNNE V. CHENEY
Humanities in America: A Report to the President, the Congress, and the American People (Washington, D.C.: NEH 1988), pp. 14, 12.

BARBARA CHRISTIAN
Reading Black, Reading Feminist, ed. Henry Louis Gates, Jr. (New York: Meridian, 1990), pp. 49, 49. "The Race for Theory," *Feminist Studies* 14 (1988): 69, 71.

CAST OF CHARACTERS

AGATHA CHRISTIE
Murder with Mirrors (New York: Dodd, Mead, 1952), p. 175.

HÉLÈNE CIXOUS
The Newly Born Woman, trans. by Betsy Wing, intro. by Sandra M. Gilbert (Minneapolis: University of Minnesota Press, 1986), pp. 75, 88, 84–85.

HILLARY RODHAM CLINTON
(Someone Who Doesn't Want to Bake Cookies)
"I'm not some little woman standing by her man like Tammy Wynette. I suppose I could have stayed home and baked cookies and had teas, but what I decided to do was fulfill my profession." Quoted in *Newsweek* (March 30, 1992): 31.

COKE CAN
As appearing in the Clarence Thomas-Anita Hill Hearings.

ALISTAIR COOKE
Former host of *Masterpiece Theatre.*

JONATHAN CULLER
Framing the Sign: Criticism and Its Institutions (Norman, Okla.: University of Oklahoma Press, 1988), pp. xvi, xii. Quoting Hillis Miller, quoting de Man, as quoted in Kimball, *Tenured Radicals,* p. 12.

CYBORGS
Donna J. Haraway, *Simians, Cyborgs, and Women: The Reinvention of Nature* (New York: Routledge, 1991), p. 181.

JACQUES DERRIDA
Spurs, trans. by Barbara Harlow (Chicago: University of Chicago Press, 1979), pp. 137, 141, 55, 57, 111; "Like the Sound of the Sea Deep within a Shell: Paul de Man's War," *Critical Inquiry* 14 (Spring 1988): 607, 623–24. Responses to "Paul de Man's War" in *Critical Inquiry* 15 (Summer 1989): Jean-Marie Apostolides, "On 'Paul de

Man's War,' " pp. 65–66; Marjorie Perloff, "Response to Jacques Derrida," pp. 767–76; Jonathan Culler, " 'Paul de Man's War' and the Aesthetic Ideology," pp. 777–83; W. Wolfgang Holdheim, "Jacques Derrida's Apologia," pp. 784–96; John Weiner, "The Responsibilities of Friendship: Jacques Derrida and Paul de Man's Collaboration," pp. 797–803; John Brenkman and Jules David Law, "Resetting the Agenda," pp. 804–11; Jacques Derrida, "Biodegradables: Seven Diary Fragments," pp. 812–73.

DENIS DONOGHUE

"A Criticism of One's Own," *Men in Feminism,* ed. Alice Jardine and Paul Smith (New York and London: Methuen, 1987), pp. 149, 151.

DINESH D'SOUZA

Illiberal Education: The Politics of Race and Sex on Campus (New York: Free Press, 1991); quoted in *The Village Voice* (June 18, 1991): 36.

DAVID DUKE

Presidential candidate-to-be, in *Newsweek* (November 18, 1991): 24–28.

ANDREA DWORKIN

Intercourse (New York: The Free Press, 1987), p. 137.

TERRY EAGLETON

Literary Theory: An Introduction (Minneapolis: University of Minnesota Press, 1983), pp. 49, 199, 200, 215, 201–2, 217, 86. Quoting Timothy Brennan, " 'Masterpiece Theatre' and the Uses of Tradition," *American Media and Mass Culture,* ed. Don Lazere (Berkeley: University of California, 1987), p. 374.

BRETT EASTON ELLIS

Notorious author.

BUCHI EMECHETTA

Head Above Water (London: Fontana, 1986), pp. 23–24.

CAST OF CHARACTERS

KAREN FINLEY
"The Constant State of Desire," in *Out From Under: Texts by Women Performance Artists,* ed. Lenora Champagne (New York: Theater Communications Group, 1990), p. 64; quoted in Luc Sante, "Blood and Chocolate," *The New Republic* (October 15, 1990): 36.

STANLEY FISH
We are indebted to Professor Fish for his first representation of himself here; quoted in Scott Heller, "A Constellation of Recently Hired Professors Illuminates the English Department at Duke," *Chronicle of Higher Education* (May 27, 1987): 13.

ELIZABETH FOX-GENOVESE
"The Claims of a Common Culture: Gender, Race, Class, and the Canon," *Salmagundi* 72 (Fall 1986): 133, 136, 134–35, 142–43.

PHYLLIS FRANKLIN
Excutive Director, Modern Language Assocation.

JANE GALLOP
The Daughter's Seduction: Feminism and Psychoanalysis (Ithaca: Cornell University Press, 1982), p. 127; *Thinking Through the Body* (New York: Columbia University Press, 1988), p. 165.

HENRY LOUIS GATES, JR.
"Authority, (White) Power, and the (Black) Critic; or, It's All Greek to Me," in *The Future of Literary Theory,* ed. Ralph Cohen (New York: Routledge, 1989), pp. 334, 336.

SANDRA M. GILBERT AND SUSAN GUBAR
The Madwoman in the Attic: The Woman Writer and the Nineteenth-Century Literary Imagination (New Haven: Yale University Press, 1979), p. 3.

ALLEN GINSBERG
Howl (San Francisco: City Lights, 1959).

Cast of Characters

GERALD GRAFF
"The Future of Theory in the Teaching of Literature," in *The Future of Literary Theory*, p. 263.

GEOFFREY HARTMAN
Saving the Text: Literature/Derrida/Philosophy (Baltimore: Johns Hopkins University Press, 1981), pp. 1, 18; "Blindness and Insight," *The New Republic* (March 7, 1988): 26.

CAROLYN HEILBRUN
"Bringing the Spirit Back to English Studies," in *Hamlet's Mother and Other Women* (New York: Ballantine, 1990), p. 206.

JESSE HELMS
Quoted in "The Right Wing's Cultural Warrior," *Newsweek* (July 2, 1990): 51. Helms quoting Pat Robertson, "Fine Art or Foul? *Newsweek* (July 2, 1990): 49. Letter of Helms (March 6, 1990) to Charles A. Bowsher, Comptroller General, Federal General Accounting Office, quoted in George Byers Jr., *Bookends* (April 1990).

E. D. HIRSCH, JR.
" 'Cultural Literacy' Does Not Mean 'Canon,' " *Salmagundi* 71 (Fall 1986): 120, 119; *Cultural Literacy: What Every American Needs to Know*, rev. ed. (New York, 1988), pp. xiv, 164, 183; with Joseph F. Kett and James Trefil, *The Dictionary of Cultural Literacy* (Boston: Houghton-Mifflin, 1988), p. 131.

CAROL IANONE
Unsuccessful candidate for NEH council; *c.v.* published in *Lingua Franca* (October 1991).

IRANIAN TERRORISTS 1, 2, and 3
"Rushdie in Hiding: An Interview," by Gerald Marzorati, *The New York Times Magazine* (November 4, 1990): 31–33, 68, 78, 84, 85.

CAST OF CHARACTERS

LUCE IRIGARAY
This Sex Which Is Not One, trans. by Catherine Porter with Carolyn Burke (Ithaca: Cornell University Press, 1985), pp. 29, 133–34; *Speculum of the Other Woman* trans. by Gilian C. Gill (Ithaca: Cornell University Press, 1985), p. 298.

JACK NICHOLSON LOOK-ALIKE
Quoting *Rolling Stone* (September 6, 1990): 60.

FREDRIC JAMESON
With James H. Kavanaugh, "The Weakest Link: Marxism in Literary Studies," *The Left Academy: Marxist Scholarship on American Campuses,* ed. Bertell Olman and Edward Vernoff (New York: McGraw-Hill, 1984), p. 3. Quoting Jean-Francois Lyotard, *The Post-Modern Condition: A Report on Knowledge,* trans. Geoff Bennington and Brian Massumi, foreword by Fredric Jameson (Minneapolis: University of Minnesota Press, 1984), p. 37.

JENNIFER
A student at Boondock State.

ERICA JONG
Famous author.

JUDY
Judith Butler, *Gender Trouble: Feminism and the Subversion of Identity* (New York: Routledge), p. 71.

ROGER KIMBALL
Tenured Radicals: How Politics Has Corrupted Our Higher Education (New York: Harper & Row, 1990), p. 142; quoted in Anne Matthews, "Deciphering Victorian Underwear and Other Seminars," *The New York Times Magazine* (February 10, 1991): 58.

Cast of Characters

STEPHEN KING

Quoted in *Kingdom of Fear: The World of Stephen King*, ed. Tim Underwood and Chuck Miller (New York: New American Library, 1986), epigraph and p. 151.

TED KOPPEL

Host of *Nightline*.

JULIA KRISTEVA

Quoted in Moi, *Sexual/Textual Politics*, p. 175; *Revolution in Poetic Language*, trans. by Margaret Waller, intro. by Leon S. Roudiez (New York: Columbia University Press, 1984), p. 30; "Stabat Mater," *Tales of Love*, trans. by Leon S. Roudiez (New York: Columbia University Press, 1987), pp. 234–35.

LANGUAGE POETS

Robert Grenier, in Ron Silliman, ed., *In the American Tree* (Orono, Maine: National Poetry Foundation, 1986), p. 496; Alan Davies, in Silliman, p. 432; Grenier, in Silliman, pp. 496, 538.

URSULA K. LE GUIN

"Text, Silence, Performance," in *Dancing at the Edge of the World: Thoughts on Words, Women, Places* (New York: Grove, 1989), p. 180.

FRANK LENTRICCHIA

Quoted in Heller, " Constellation," 12.

DAVID LODGE

Quoted in *Publisher's Weekly* (August 18, 1989): 41; *Times Ed. Supp.* (May 18, 1990): Bll; quoting Morris Zapp in *Small World* (New York: Macmillan, 1985), p. 328.

SHIRLEY MACLAINE

Going Within: A Guide for Inner Transformation (New York: Bantam, 1989), pp. 274, 285, and "the Chakric System Chart."

CAST OF CHARACTERS

MADONNA
Quoted in Don Shewey, "The Gospel According to St. Madonna," *The Advocate* 577 (May 21, 1991): 41.

NORMAN MAILER
Quoted in Richard Stern, "Penned In," *Critical Inquiry* 13 (August 1986): 21; J. Lennon, ed., *Conversations with Norman Mailer* (Jackson and London: University of Mississippi Press, 1988), pp. 344, 286, 279; Mailer, *The Prisoner of Sex* (New York: Signet, 1971) p. 36; Mailer, "The Writer's Imagination and the Imagination of the State," in *The New York Review of Books* (February 13, 1986): 24.

IMELDA MARCOS
Former first lady of the Philippines.

JANE MARPLE
Niece of Agatha Christie's Jane Marple; heroine of "Masterpiece Theatre."

J. HILLIS MILLER
Quoted in Kimball, "The Academy Debates the Canon," pp. 36, 35.

TORIL MOI
Sexual/Textual Politics: Feminist Literary Theory (London: Methuen, 1985), pp. 66–67, 170, 63.

TONI MORRISON
"Unspeakable Things Unspoken: The Afro-American Presence in American Literature," *Michigan Quarterly Review* (Winter 1989): 5.

BHARATI MUKHERJEE
In "An Interview with Bharati Mukherjee," *The Iowa Review* 20, 3 (Fall 1990): 18, 29.

JOYCE CAROL OATES
Famous author.

Cast of Characters

RICHARD OHMANN
Politics of Letters (Middletown, Conn.: Wesleyan University Press, 1987), pp. 232, 14.

CAMILLE PAGLIA
Sexual Personae: Art and Decadence from Nefertiti to Emily Dickinson (New Haven: Yale University Press, 1990), pp. 21, 21; quoted in *New York* (March 4, 1991): 30, 26; *Sexual Personae,* pp. 92, 37–38.

PLAGIARISM PANEL
See James Atlas, "When an Original Idea Sounds Really Familiar," *New York Times* (July 28, 1991): E2.

HERCULE POIROT
Famed international detective created by Agatha Christie; on resistance journalism, quoting *Critical Inquiry* 14, 3 (Spring 1988): 652. Quoted by Jane Marple, from Agatha Christie, *Murder on the Orient Express,* in *5 Complete Hercule Poirot Novels* (New York: Avenel, 1986), p. 250.

MARILYN QUAYLE
(Someone Shouting About Family Values)
Wife of former vice president.

DAN RATHER
CBS newscaster.

NANCY REAGAN
Former first lady.

ISHMAEL REED
Author of *Mumbo Jumbo, Reckless Eyeballing,* and *Writin' Is Fightin'.*

RHIZOMES
Gilles Deleuze, "Rhizomes Versus Trees," *The Deleuze Reader,* ed. and intro. by Constantin V. Boundas (New York: Columbia University Press, 1993), p. 35.

CAST OF CHARACTERS

ADRIENNE RICH

"North American Time," in *The Fact of a Doorframe: Poems Selected and New 1959–1984* (New York: Norton, 1984), p. 325; "Compulsory Heterosexuality and the Lesbian Continuum," in *Blood, Bread, and Poetry: Selected Prose 1979–1985* (New York: Norton, 1986), p. 47.

LILLIAN S. ROBINSON

"Canon Fathers and Myth Universe," in *The Future of Literary Theory*, p. 263.

JOANNA RUSS

"Pornography by Women, for Women, with Love," in *Magic Mommas, Trembling Sisters, Puritans, and Perverts* (Trumansburg, New York: Crossing Press, 1985), pp. 90, 96.

EDWARD SAID

The World, the Text, and the Critic (Cambridge, Mass.: Harvard University Press, 1983), pp. 43, 50; "Intellectuals in the Post-Colonial World," *Salmagundi* 70–71 (Spring-Summer 1986): 44, 50, 52; "Representing the Colonized: Anthropology's Interlocutors," *Critical Inquiry* 15 (Winter 1989): 216–17. "An Ideology of Difference," *Critical Inquiry* 12 (Autumn 1985): 38–56. Responses to Said in *Critical Inquiry* 15 (Spring 1989): Robert J. Griffin, "Ideology and Misrepresentation: A Response to Edward Said," pp. 611–25; Daniel Boyarin and Jonathan Boyarin, "Toward a Dialogue with Edward Said," pp. 626–33; Edward Said, "Response," pp. 634–46.

ROBERT SCHOLES

"Aiming a Canon at the Curriculum," *Salmagundi* 72 (Fall 1986): 116, 103, 113, 104; quoting J. Talmadge Wright, dissertation abstract (University of California, Irvine, 1985), cited in Charles J. Sykes, *ProfScam*, p. 187.

SCOTT

A student at Boondock State.

Cast of Characters

EVE KOSOFSKY SEDGWICK
"The Beast in the Closet: James and the Writing of Homosexual Panic," in *Speaking of Gender,* ed. Elaine Showalter (New York: Routledge, 1989), p. 243.

BARBARA HERRNSTEIN SMITH
Quoted in Anthony Saville, "But Some Books Are Still Bad," *New York Times Book Review* 4 (June 4, 1989): 35; *Contingencies of Value: Alternative Perspectives for Critical Theory* (Cambridge, Mass.: Harvard University Press, 1988), pp. 183, 175.

GAYATRI SPIVAK
In Other Words: Essays in Cultural Politics (New York: Methuen, 1987), pp. 15, 28, 214, 26, 221, 241, 215, 82. On the ontology of farts, see "Acting Bits/Identity Talk," *Critical Inquiry* (Summer 1992): 797. On the discourse of the clitoris, see "Translator's Preface," Jacques Derrida, *Of Grammatology* (Baltimore: Johns Hopkins University Press, 1976), p. lxvi.

DANIELLE STEEL
Dedication to *Star* (New York: Dell Publishers, 1989).

GEORGE STEINER
Real Presences: Is There Anything in What We Say? (London: Faber and Faber, 1989), pp. 33, 32, 67, 68, 207.

CATHARINE STIMPSON
Chronicle of Higher Education 37, 4 (1990): B2.

CHARLES J. SYKES
ProfScam: Professors and the Demise of Higher Education (Washington, D.C., 1988), pp. 115, 51, 264.

JANE P. TOMPKINS
"Sentimental Power: *Uncle Tom's Cabin* and the Politics of Literary History," *The New Feminist Criticism: Essays on Women, Litera-*

CAST OF CHARACTERS

ture, and Theory, ed. Elaine Showalter (New York: Pantheon, 1985), p. 84.

HELEN VENDLER
"Feminism and Literature," *New York Review of Books* (May 31, 1990): 19, 23, 24, 22. *The Odes of John Keats* (Cambridge, Mass.: 1983), pp. 145, 296.

VOICE-OVER RAPPER
"Department of Higher Education [from a flyer distributed by the Rapola Company of Colton, California]," quoted in *The New Yorker* (October 7, 1991): 102.

ALICE WALKER
"Coral and Turquoise," *The New Statesman* (September 15, 1989): 13.

DR. RUTH WESTHEIMER
Internationally known sexologist.

About the Authors

If Sandra M. Gilbert and Susan Gubar were not born to write about this subject, they have been socially constructed to explore it. Coauthors of *The Madwoman in the Attic* and its three-volume sequel, *No Man's Land*, co-editors of the *Norton Anthology of Literature by Women*, and individually or together responsible for a range of other texts, both have professed literature and literacy in a range of institutional settings, including the School of Criticism and the Indiana Women's Prison as well as the University of California, Davis; Indiana University; Princeton University; Tufts University; the University of Illinois, Chicago Circle; the California State University, Hayward; and several NEH Summer Seminars for College Teachers. Gubar has chaired the English Institute's Board of Supervisors and Gilbert is currently an officer of the Modern Language Association.